Immersive Arts Integration

This step-by-step guide takes you through the process of transitioning your K-8 school to the Immersive Arts Integration model. The model develops deeper connections with content, stronger relationships, and a positive school climate. Co-authors Dr. Jennifer Katona and Dr. Jennifer Masone combine decades of educational and artistic expertise to share a four-year roadmap to a sustainable immersive arts approach to teaching and learning. The Immersive Arts Integration model is based on five key tenets: Building Ensemble; Arts Integration into Core Content Instruction; Creating Integrated Units of Study; Elevating the Role of the Arts Specialist; and Spaces and Places. The authors explore each concept and its implementation, as well as measurable outcomes pertaining to pedagogy, academic achievement, social emotional learning, equity, multilingual learning, facilities usage, and school climate. They include resources for stakeholders across the educational spectrum to utilize and provide considerations for different staffing and fiscal models. Articulated schedules of professional development, lesson plan templates, sample lessons, and sample unit plans are also included for immediate use. Whether you are a district or school administrator or working in the classroom, you can have a hand in gaining buy-in and implementing an educational model that both infuses the arts into daily instruction and creates lasting improvement within your institution.

Jennifer Katona is Executive Director of the Educational Theatre Association, USA, and co-director of the Immersive Arts Integration.

Jennifer Masone is Principal at Cranbury Elementary School, USA, and co-director for the Immersive Arts Integration.

Also Available from Routledge Eye on Education
(www.routledge.com/eyeoneducation)

Integrating Creative Movement and Theater Across the K-6 Curriculum: Moving Through the School Day
Kelly Mancini Becker

Everyday STEAM for the Early Childhood Classroom: Integrating the Arts into STEM Teaching
Margaret Loring Merrill

Learning Through Movement in the K-6 Classroom: Integrating Theatre and Dance to Achieve Educational Equity
Kelly Mancini Becker

Let's Stop Teaching and Start Designing Learning: A Practical Guide
Jason Kennedy

Do Your Lessons Love Your Students? Creative Education for Social Change
Mariah Rankine-Landers and Jessa Brie Moreno

Enlivening Instruction with Drama and Improv: A Guide for Second Language and World Language Teachers
Melisa Cahnmann-Taylor and Kathleen McGovern

The A in STEAM: Lesson Plans and Activities for Integrating Art, Ages 0–8
Jerilou J. Moore and Kerry P. Holmes

Let's Stop Teaching and Start Designing Learning: A Practical Guide
Jason Kennedy

Immersive Arts Integration

A Step-by-Step Guide to Transitioning Your K-8 School

Jennifer Katona and Jennifer Masone

Taylor & Francis Group

NEW YORK AND LONDON

Designed cover image: © Getty Images

First published 2025
by Routledge
605 Third Avenue, New York, NY 10158

and by Routledge
4 Park Square, Milton Park, Abingdon, Oxon, OX14 4RN

Routledge is an imprint of the Taylor & Francis Group, an informa business

© 2025 Jennifer Katona and Jennifer Masone

The right of Jennifer Katona and Jennifer Masone to be identified as authors of this work has been asserted in accordance with sections 77 and 78 of the Copyright, Designs and Patents Act 1988.

All rights reserved. No part of this book may be reprinted or reproduced or utilised in any form or by any electronic, mechanical, or other means, now known or hereafter invented, including photocopying and recording, or in any information storage or retrieval system, without permission in writing from the publishers.

Trademark notice: Product or corporate names may be trademarks or registered trademarks, and are used only for identification and explanation without intent to infringe.

ISBN: 978-1-032-79211-8 (hbk)
ISBN: 978-1-032-79207-1 (pbk)
ISBN: 978-1-003-49343-3 (ebk)

DOI: 10.4324/9781003493433

Typeset in Palatino
by Apex CoVantage, LLC

Contents

Meet the Authors vi
Preface viii

1 Theory of Practice 1

2 Foundational Work 20

3 Ensemble Building 36

4 Arts Integration into Core Content Instruction 56

5 Creating Integrated Units of Study 83

6 Elevating the Role of the Arts Teacher 97

7 Spaces and Places 108

8 Implementation in Action 120

References 136

Meet the Authors

Dr. Jennifer Katona, Ph.D., is the current Executive Director of the Educational Theatre Association and President of the Educational Theatre Foundation, where she works to serve theatre educators across the United States and Canada with comprehensive resources to build, support, and sustain their theatre programs. Dr. Katona is also the President of 3 Looms Creative Education Consulting, which serves as program manager for the NYC DoE Filmed Theatre Partnership with the National Theatre, London, and the Connecticut expansion of the Arthur Miller Foundation theatre teacher development program. Dr. Katona is the former Founder and Director of the Graduate Program in Educational Theatre at The City College of New York, CUNY, where she developed and taught Curriculum Development, Theatre Directing Foundations, Arts Integration, and Student Teaching Seminar. Jennifer holds a Ph.D. in Urban Education: Arts Policy, and her current research explores factors that influence the decision of a school leader to maintain or eliminate arts programming in their school and building sustainable arts programming in urban schools. Jennifer has spoken and presented on this topic at many conferences across the country.

Dr. Jennifer Masone, Ed.D., has over 25 years of experience working with children of all ages and is passionate about improving outcomes for all children. She currently serves as the Principal of Cranbury Elementary School. Prior to that, she served as the Interim Principal of Nathan Hale Middle School and Principal of Wolfpit Elementary School. She has experience in both urban and suburban school districts, where she was an administrator and teacher. She is passionate about all art forms and their ability to bridge pedagogy and content by engaging students while transcending language, socioeconomic status, and other barriers that may typically hinder the educational process. She also has an extensive aquatics background and a keen interest in saving children's lives and changing the way society approaches educating children on water safety awareness. She has an Ed.D. in Educational Leadership. Dr. Masone is also the Co-Director of Immersive Arts Integration, an arts-based school improvement model.

Preface

Dream Big.

We're so glad you're here with us! Thank you for opening up this book and joining us on the journey to Dream Big. It is our hope that after you read this book, you will be able to make shifts in your school that will positively impact your students, staff, and communities and ultimately make the world a better place.

Let's be clear about two things. First, arts integration is not a new concept. Lots of folks are integrating the arts in meaningful ways in schools around the world. They should keep going. This book does not to take away from any arts integration efforts but rather adds to them. Second, emotional connections are an integral part of humanity and of the learning process. In recent years, the focus on technology has had a positive and negative impact on students. Let's keep and celebrate the positive aspects that help to unify, enlighten, and challenge our students. But, we must actively work to counteract how technology results in disconnection and isolation among and between people. Ultimately, it is our ability to connect with one another and celebrate one another's humanity that will yield to the advancement of fairness, tolerance, and an educated people.

The Immersive Arts Integration model celebrates the most powerful resource we all possess: our VOICE. This model is founded on the principle that everyone has a unique voice and that one's voice will be elevated and celebrated as a result of one's educational experience. This concept organically ensures that inclusivity, respect, and connectedness are part of the daily experiences of all participants in the educational process. It serves as an antidote to an educational system that sometimes leads students and teachers to be compliant, passive, and disconnected from content. Instead, they are actively involved in crafting their learning and demonstrating it. Too often, students are told to use their voice but not taught how to do it. Let's teach them!

Imagine a school that looks, feels, and sounds like the people who are in it. And because the people who are in it are free to express themselves in a variety of ways academically, socially, emotionally, and artistically, they are enthusiastic and engaged. The students look one another in the eyes when they speak; they proudly share their learning; they advocate for what they need to learn. The staff is excited to teach; they have worked with one another to craft their units; they stand with students in the circle and facilitate learning. The halls are filled with music, and the walls are filled with art. Challenges are met with support and caring. The energy is electric. This is possible. This is Immersive Arts Integration.

You come to this book with your own perspective. You may be an artist, a teacher, an administrator, a community arts foundation member, or even a student. But you know the situation you're in needs to change. The book is generally told from the perspective of the administrator and from the perspective of a visiting artist. If you are neither of these, you will still see yourself in the work. Just keep looking.

Let's talk about change in general. If you've been an administrator in education long enough, you will have witnessed short-lived attempts at school reform. You know the kind . . . someone at the central office tells the principal the school is going to have a STEM focus or an engineering focus or a culinary focus. There are half-hearted attempts to train unenthusiastic teachers. Some teachers will love it; some will say they're going along with it but silently protest; and some will thrive on sarcastically critiquing every step of the process. Top-down rarely works. Bottom-up rarely works. An evenly distributed commitment to change yields the most conducive working environment, and we'll walk you through the process. Then there's the issue of time. How successful is a change effort if it takes a decade? With intentional planning and a focus on coming to a consensus, the work will flourish. The intent is to establish a self-sustaining model in four years.

If you have been in arts education long enough, you have been a part of a great many efforts to impact school reform through arts integration one classroom at a time. After a few years of successful one-off residencies with a wonderful partner teacher in the building, the principal thinks it might be time to roll the work out to the whole grade or a cluster of teachers. If you are a successful resident artist in the field, you can remain in a school in isolated classrooms year after year after year. But, this only impacts the students who participate; it does not impact the whole school. For students to fully grasp the method of arts-integrated instruction, it cannot be something they come in contact with sporadically for 12 weeks a year in one or two classes in one or two grades. The work needs to be implemented in the full school experience–from the hallways to classrooms, gymnasium, playground, and cafeteria.

This book will walk you through the steps to transition your school to a fully Immersive Arts Integration model. There are five key components of the model:

- Ensemble Building
- Arts Integration into Core Content Instruction
- Creating Integrated Units of Study
- Elevating the Role of the Arts Teachers
- Spaces and Places

The five tenets are embedded within the chapters of the book in such a way as to guide you in your own process, challenge you to think about what your current school has and may not have, and think critically about what is important to your school community. Here is a brief summary of each chapter:

Chapter 1: Theory of Practice

This chapter provides the underlying theories of practice for the success of the work. It offers the reader a comprehensive look at the research that supports the value of an arts education, both the intrinsic and extrinsic benefits. The leading research in the field of Arts Education supports the positive impact of the arts on brain development, academic achievement, and social emotional learning. Leadership theory is also discussed to prepare the administrator for the transition process.

Chapter 2: Foundational Work

This chapter outlines what needs to be done by the school team to prepare the teachers, students, and community for this shift. The chapter will discuss how to engage family, students, staff, and the community to evolve the organization. Critical components such as budget, communication, scheduling, and professional development will be discussed.

Chapters 3–7: The 5 Tenets

These chapters explore the five key tenets of the model. They define each tenet, outline the professional development that needs to take place, touch on anticipated challenges, and inspire you to consider how you might accomplish the work, given your unique circumstances.

Chapter 8: Implementation in Action

This chapter tells the story of the model's development and includes real-world examples of misconceptions, how to engage the whole school community, and how to identify successful early outcomes based on the implementation of this work, including both academic and social-emotional learning.

It is our hope that this approach provides school communities with a roadmap to either the introduction or reintroduction of the arts to bolster the educational offerings for a school that is already successful or to provide a method of school evolution for school communities to navigate the given circumstances of the current educational landscape. We hope you enjoy the book and find it useful in your journey to improve teaching and learning outcomes in your educational organization!

1

Theory of Practice

> In writing, we would write a page on a topic like a biography or an animal topic. Then we do a theatre activity where you can act out your character or do a tableau about your story writing. It's fun, we get to move our bodies, we can stretch, and I wish we did it more. It's so fun. **4th Grade Student**

This chapter will provide you with both context and a foundational understanding of the theory behind the Immersive Arts Integration model. We characterize both the model and the path to full implementation as key components to evolve your educational organizations. This evolution takes place as the staff, students, and community work collectively to enhance their understanding of Immersive Arts Integration and ways in which it most effectively serves the teaching and learning in the organization. First, let's talk about the benefits of the work and the theory of practice. Let's talk about what arts integration IS and what it is not. Right off the top, let us agree that Immersive Arts Integration is NOT every kid reciting Shakespeare or acting like molecules floating in the air (although that is an effective tool for learning). Immersive Arts Integration is the **how** of the instruction, not the what of the school curriculum. It is truly about elevating the artistic process and layering it on the learning process for students. This book will provide examples and instructions, but in the end, it's about the process of organically and creatively looking at the world as the primary vehicle through which we educate our students.

Immersive Arts Integration provides value to the school leaders and, in turn, the school staff. School leaders are always looking for ways to help their teachers improve their practice.

The majority of teaching rubrics place a high value on student engagement as related to academic performance. By design, Immersive Arts Integration is a fast route to outstanding instructional practice. Educators have to approach their teaching in a deep and complex way. They craft learning tasks so that students are engaged in thinking and learning both physically and cognitively. If this is feeling a bit nebulous, rest assured that we will explore the lesson plan format and ensemble work more deeply, the structure of the class, the focus on learner-centered curriculum, the intentional use of transitions and questioning, as well as the way classrooms are physically set up so that teachers engage their students at a higher level. Read on.

The Immersive Arts Integration model provides space for the human experience while achieving the expected curricular goals. This work also allows all students equitable access to the content. When a piece of art is introduced as the catalyst for discussion, students need no prior knowledge to hold an aesthetic opinion. This entry point to classwork provides instant confidence for students that propels learning. It also levels the playing field in terms of their background knowledge. Students aren't negatively impacted by a lack of life experience, nor is there a negative impact of an imbalance of life experience between students.

Let's review some key vocabulary, concepts, and foundational ideas to get you started.

Arts, Integration, and Immersive Arts Integration

Simple Definitions to Set the Stage

Simply put, **Arts Education** is the skill-based study of Visual Arts, Theatre, Dance, Music (both choral and instrumental), and Media Arts. Skill-based arts education is the discipline and skill required for a student to complete an artistic task. An acting student must understand given circumstances and motivation to act out a scene; a visual arts student must understand the elements of design to complete a perspective drawing.

Arts Integration happens when the skills-based arts education and the standard curriculum are paired in intentional and meaningful ways. This typically means the arts teacher pushes into the classroom and adds an arts component to augment the task. For example, students are learning about George Washington. The classroom teacher has them read several primary sources in order to write a paper to present to their audience. The art teacher would support them by helping students create the poster, and the music teacher would support them by teaching them a related song to sing.

Immersive Arts Integration happens when the artistic process is used as the primary vehicle through which the standard curriculum is learned. This means the classroom teacher uses the theatre process, and the arts teachers will provide support as necessary. For example, students would read about George Washington and then devise a script to become him either in a performance or living museum. The art teacher would support with costumes, props, or set, and the music teacher would support with a related song as necessary.

<u>This is a profound shift in pedagogy and is the basis for the Immersive Arts Integration model. The model and path to its full realization in your school setting are discussed throughout the rest of the book.</u>

Historical Context of Arts Education in American Schools

History, Legislation, and the Pandemic

Let's start with a bit of context regarding the evolution of arts education, legislation, and the pandemic. For most students, and as far back as the very beginning of public American schooling, there was a form of skill-based arts education embedded in the school day.

Educational pioneers such as Horace Mann, John Dewey, and Frederick Froebel all expressed the importance of the study of arts in a student's day. At that time, an arts education included singing hymns, reading great works of literature aloud, studying influential painters, and listening to classical music. A strong foundation in the study of the arts helped students develop an appreciation for the aesthetics of the arts around them.

During the first half of the 20th century, many schoolchildren encountered music and visual arts as a routine part of their school day.

As educational research evolved, so did our collective understanding of arts education. Arts educator Elliot Eisner's 1998 text *Does Experience in the Arts Boost Academic Achievement* states arts should not be included in the curriculum simply as a means of improving academic achievement, claiming that the goals of reading and mathematics are not distinctively artistic. Relating the value of an arts education only to its effect on test scores tends to undermine the value of the unique contributions of the arts to the education of the young (Eisner, 1998). Eisner outlined three hierarchical tiers for the outcomes of arts education. The first tier, arts-based outcomes, is directly related to the subject matter that an arts curriculum is designed to teach. The second tier, arts-related outcomes, discusses the perception and comprehension of aesthetic features in the general environment, such as understanding of culture, history, and aesthetic qualities in the outside world. The third tier, known as ancillary outcomes, consists of skills within arts that are transferable to non-arts tasks. Generally, ancillary outcomes are the effects on student performance in reading, math, or other academic subjects. Eisner cautions researchers and educators that ancillary outcomes are not the only outcomes that are important in adopting extensive arts curriculums in schools (Eisner, 1998). He identifies his own set of outcomes for arts education, which pertain to the dispositions that are difficult to assess but appear to be cultivated through programs that engage students in the process of artistic creation. They are a willingness to imagine possibilities that are not now but which might become; a desire to explore ambiguity, to be willing to forestall premature closure in pursuing resolutions; and the ability to recognize and accept the multiple perspectives and resolutions that work in the arts celebrate (Eisner, 1998).

The educational field was also impacted by evolving legislation. The No Child Left Behind (NCLB) Act was signed into law in 2001. It used standardized testing of literacy and math as a key measurement to demonstrate performance. The unintended consequence of the act was that it eliminated many school-based arts programs. In 2015, the Every Child Succeeds Act replaced NCLB. Though the Act still required proficiency testing on accountability goals, accountability systems, and standardized testing, it also placed the arts at the center of defining a well-rounded education for all students. Since 2015, schools across the country have been working to reinstate quality skill-based arts education programs. Working with the local government to ensure that arts instruction is taught by certified teachers and that students are receiving access to that arts education. This resulted in schools reconsidering Arts Integration in the context of modern classrooms. Arts Integration was seen as the way to get the arts into the school day. It was the answer to the leadership who would shake the budget pages saying they would love to offer music or theatre, but they could not afford another full-time staff member or the district leader who would question how they could offer theatre when the students' reading scores were so low. Arts educators often would remind a school that they could teach both art and a content area for you. They would pitch teaching drama and ensure students would learn to read at the same time. While such claims were well-intentioned and perhaps true in some pockets, ultimately, they were not helping either field push the work forward but rather diluting two.

The onset of the COVID-19 pandemic in the spring of 2020 caused the country's approach to education to shift drastically. In an attempt to ameliorate the potential spread of the virus, districts instituted mitigation factors such as universal indoor masking, isolation, quarantine, and social distancing (CDC, 2022). Many schools also shifted to online learning for a period of time. While these factors may have saved lives, they impacted the educational experience of children. Years later, we are still understanding the impact these drastic measures had on the academic and social emotional learning of students. The Department of Education acknowledged, "Nearly all students have experienced some challenges to their mental health and well-being during the pandemic . . . with early research showing disparities based on race, ethnicity, LGBTQ+ identity, and other factors" (2021).

The pandemic had the unintended consequence of demonstrating how critical human connectivity is to child development and education. Post pandemic, we know how imperative it is that we craft student experiences to counteract the impact social distancing continues to have on our students and foster human connectivity as a baseline for the educational experience.

The Immersive Arts Integration model enters the educational landscape as a natural evolution from the historical, legislative, and post-pandemic factors of the last hundred or so years. It marries what we value about a well-rounded education and what we know to be essential about the educational experience. Now, let's talk about the impact of the arts on students.

Impact on Brain Development

Using the Arts to Ensure Effective Learning

As you probably suspect, arts are good for the brain! Studies have been conducted correlating higher test scores for those students who encountered the arts in their schooling. Neuroscience and brain research have been done to support the connection between the power of the arts and the development of a child. Cumulatively, the research articulates how students' strongest weapon is their ability to think creatively and that imagination is a skill, just as any other, in need of training and development. Piaget's widely accepted theory of assimilation and accommodation is rooted in the belief that this function occurs through the creative process. Piaget saw assimilation and accommodation, mechanisms of the development of thought, as mechanisms underlying the creative process (Ayman-Nolley, 1999, p. 268). Research by Zull and Kolb supports the integration of these domains in development, as do many previous theories of learning from pioneers such as Vygotsky, Piaget, Dewey, and Gardner. A 1999 study in Chicago Public Schools by Catterall and Waldorf provides strong support for arts education but falls short on its implementation of scope and sequence and required hours.

James Zull (2002) shared his research on the brain with the release of The Art of Changing the Brain, which builds on Piaget's earlier notion. Zull lists four essential components to changing the brain for effective learning to occur: practice, emotion, problem solving, and engagement. His research indicates that when a teacher dispenses with explaining everything to a student, it frees the student's brain to experience the emotions necessary for effective change to occur. When the teacher does not explain information to the students, it transfers the power from the teacher back to the student; studies in neuroscience tell us that positive emotions in learning are generated when the student is able to generate ideas on his or her own (p. 70). This process occurs in the frontal cortex of the brain, which is also responsible for voluntary movements. "Voluntary movements of course are owned or chosen. The biochemical rewards of learning are not provided by explanation but by student ownership" (p. 72). The final element to changing the brain for effective learning is to engage the entire brain, specifically in the four regions of the cerebral cortex.

So what does this mean? Simply put, if educators can engage all four areas, then more neurons will fire, and more networks will be created, which is the key to deeper learning. Immersive Arts Integration fits the Zull cycle perfectly – particularly the study of theatre. It is in the nature of the theatrical rehearsal process for student actors to take a script and practice their role: blocking (identifying the location and movements of actors) and interacting with other actors. Through the process of getting into character, they are asked to evoke and connect to the emotions of the character they are playing. Throughout the rehearsal process, they are asked to problem solve situations that arise (typically when blocking is not working or is too complicated). In these cases, they are called upon to make critical decisions. The entire process of putting on a theatrical performance requires the student actor to be fully present and fully engaged.

Zull's work is based heavily on the work of psychologist David Kolb (1984) and his cycle of learning theory, which addresses teaching to the whole brain. His cycle of learning theory includes four steps that correspond with the four areas of the cortex. The cycle includes: 1) experience – gathering information through experiencing the situation with our senses in the sensory cortex, 2) reflection – making sense of the experience through the back integrative cortex, 3) abstraction – making meaning out of the information and creating personal connections through the front integrative cortex, and 4) active testing – acting on the ideas through the motor cortex. Again, the Immersive Arts Integration model fully aligns with the neurological process Kolb lays out.

To fully illustrate the connections between the educational theorists and the Immersive Arts Integration model, let us use an arts integration learning experience from a 6th-grade study of the Industrial Revolution. In this example, students are asked to take on the role of factory workers working on an assembly line, making wooden cars and airplanes, which would then be sold as a class fundraiser. Through this process, students "experience" the Industrial Revolution by gathering information and experiencing the situation with their senses. Moving beyond reading about a factory worker's account to being able to simulate the experience in a role is a powerful shift. They then make sense of the experience of being in a certain enterprise or field by simulating the various trials of an industrial factory worker. Their character may get injured or sick, and they have to reflect on how they would move forward in those circumstances. Through teacher-directed questions after each experience, the students can make personal meaning and connections. As an out-of-role extension, a teacher may ask students to think about a time they, too, had to overcome a challenge or to consider how they would feel if, at their age, they were responsible for financially supporting their family. To complete Kolb's four-part process, the students put their learning into action by being asked to sell the wooden cars and planes at a local market and are keenly aware through the process that the money made will support their family. The critical element to teaching is student engagement in the curriculum and the power of the learning experience for the student.

Dewey states in <u>Arts as Experience</u> (1934) that, often, educational experiences for students are unclear, both in their meaning and purpose. He argues that a true experience occurs when it reaches fulfillment in the student: "[W]e have an experience when the material experience runs its course to fulfillment. Then, and only then, is it integrated within and demarcated in the general stream of experience from other experiences" (p. 37). Dewey defines fulfillment as the point where the learning experience has reached a natural ending; "the process (the experience) continues until a mutual adaptation of the self and the object emerges and that particular experience comes to a close" (p. 45). Using the 6th grade Industrial Revolution example to illustrate Dewey's thinking in a modern context, students know the inner workings of factory life and can speak as experts on the intricacies of the work. They were committed to the role, and when the unit ended, they had reached fulfillment and indeed had engaged in a lasting learning experience. The inclusion of arts education naturally encompasses the learning cycle of both Kolb and Zull and provides the learning experience that is necessary for deep learning, as Dewey suggests.

With the emphasis on standardized testing scores as the defining measure of students', schools', and districts' success, the arts have increasingly and erroneously been cast aside as the means to the achievement end. As indicated, the inclusion of the arts encompasses the cycle of learning as a brain-based experience. We posit that the arts *can* not only be included to support the learning of core content but *should* be included to support the learning of core content.

Impact on Social Emotional Components

Social Emotional Learning, Creativity, and Peer Relationships

Well before the pandemic put most American students and teachers behind screens, the need for supporting students' social emotional learning (SEL) was a high priority for schools. Schools are inherently social places and have both structured and unstructured environments where interactions take place. It is important for our littlest learners to develop skills early in life and to thrive in positive learning environments. "Research shows that SEL not only improves achievement by 11 percentile points, but it also increases prosocial behaviors (such as kindness, sharing, and empathy), improves student attitudes toward school, and reduces depression and stress among students" (Durlak et al., 2011).

The leading framework and resource for schools on Social Emotional Learning is the Collaborative for Academic, Social, and Emotional Learning (CASEL), which defines SEL as

> the process through which all young people and adults acquire and apply the knowledge, skills, and attitudes to develop healthy identities, manage emotions and achieve personal and collective goals, feel and show empathy for others, establish and maintain supportive relationships, and make responsible and caring decisions.

These processes take place internally/individually and externally/socially. CASEL identifies five areas of focus:

Self-Awareness, Self-Management, Social Awareness, Relationship Skills, and Responsible Decision Making. A foundational concept in arts education is knowing one's own thoughts and perspectives then applying them to view or participate in the artistic or creative process.

When art becomes a shared process, students are accessing their relationship skills. Asking students to look each other in the eye and ask about their day or share their opinion on a story or recently learned fact is powerful. When students view a work of art and then engage in conversation about it, it requires them to have a deep understanding of their own feelings and then be able to communicate those to a peer. When students are tasked with participating in an ensemble game, collaborating on a devised script, or responding to peer questions in the role of a character, they have the opportunity to practice the five areas of focus in meaningful ways as related to the curriculum. These tasks naturally align with CASEL's areas of focus and will yield positive outcomes.

Another foundational part of the artistic process is the creation of art. This is most closely aligned with the self-management aspect of the CASEL framework. It is important for students to be able to manage their own emotions and use stress management strategies. The artistic process is often used to this end. When students are creating their own art, the creative process can serve as both a form of self-expression and a distraction from challenging feelings (Drake & Winner, 2012). Effectively managing challenging feelings will create space and time for students to focus on other content areas, such as reading and writing.

Impact on Life Skills

21st Century Learning
At the turn of the century, educators, leaders, academics, and governmental agencies identified the knowledge and skills necessary to meet the demands of the vast social, cultural, and economic changes our nation and the world was experiencing. These skills, also called the Four C's, include: 1) Critical Thinking, 2) Creative Thinking, 3) Collaborating, and 4) Communicating. In order for students to achieve these skills, teachers must understand how to craft learning experiences that yield those results.

Often, in a traditional teaching model, the teacher presents information to the students, the facts are memorized, and perhaps a low-level impact question is asked. For example, math teachers traditionally teach the concept of slope and plot data points on a grid using the X/Y axis either on a whiteboard or computer and determine student understanding by their performance on a worksheet or computer question. Students may engage in some critical thinking if the questions are challenging, but, in most cases, the 4 C's are not used.

Using an Immersive Arts Integration approach with this same example, students are brought to the school cafeteria to create their own X, Y grid using blue painter's tape on the floor tiles. Students can complete a series of activities, placing them inside the grid. They can work in small groups to ask peers to show their answers by standing on a grid point or using a bean bag to toss on a grid point and then name it. In the second example, the students' conceptual learning is the same; however, the process of learning and the demonstration of understanding are different. Learning is enhanced by students *becoming* points on the grid and interacting in a physical way with the grid itself. For obvious reasons, it's also just more fun to walk a grid than to sit at a desk.

The key component to preparing students for the 21st century is to place them in situations where they have to process information critically and think creatively to solve those problems as they communicate and collaborate with their peers. This corresponds to the creative process beautifully, as artists are always in the midst of solving a creative problem. In the theatre, all staff, including the lighting designers, prop and costume designers, and the director, come together with one common goal: *What would best serve the story?* In Immersive Arts Integration, all content areas come together with their units of study and lesson objectives with one common goal: *What would best serve student learning?*

Impact on Diversity, Equity, and Inclusion

How the Model Supports All Stakeholders

The United States continues to be a diverse country with many groups of people who all have access to public education. Groups of people could be based on race, ethnicity, color, sex, gender, gender identity, sexual identity, socioeconomic status, language, culture, national origin, religion/spirituality, age, (dis)ability, to name a few. All people share identities among multiple groups. If you want to do a deep dive into current populations in K-12 public schools, check out The National Center for Education Statistics. You'll find that the numbers suggest our schools continue to be diverse places based on many metrics. As a result, it is important that schools address the need for equity and inclusion of all groups.

In short, diversity refers to how people differ; equity refers to all groups' access to fair and just (not necessarily equal) treatment, and inclusion refers to the act of welcoming and supporting all groups. There are currently no national DEI standards for K-12 schools, but many states and school districts are implementing their own measures. The National Core Arts Standards also do not directly reference DEI standards (they are currently being developed), though they do share inclusion guidelines for students with disabilities.

For the purposes of this discussion, it is important to acknowledge how the Immersive Arts Integration model creates space and opportunity for all groups to be welcomed, have access, and be represented. The model is intentionally designed to place the individual learner's (both child and adult) experience and connection with content at the center of the educational process. As you'll learn in Chapter 3, both children and adults start their day in an ensemble circle so that all voices have equal value. When they observe and comment on a work of art, they are doing so from their experience. Their socioeconomic status is no longer a barrier because the approach from their perspective and all perspectives are valued. Their disabilities are incorporated into their responses because they are a reflection of their identity and not separate from their identity. Each learner is celebrated and valued in the model.

Organizational Change Theories

Steps to Lead the Change

Whether you decide to launch a focus on Immersive Arts Integration for school improvement purposes or to ensure a well-rounded educational experience for your school community, it will be a change. Leadership's ability to manage the change will directly impact the success and sustainability of that change. It is beneficial to understand the research relative to both organizational change management models and school improvement models. Understanding the two approaches and perspectives can provide a broader context for understanding the work established in this book. This section will explore the theories and their impact on Immersive Arts Integration.

When planning for a significant shift like Immersive Arts Integration, leaders may consider the work of McKinsey, the ADKAR model, or Kotter's 8 Step Process to Accelerate Change. These models provide a comprehensive approach to leading change and include elements of pre-planning, structural change, implementation, reflection, and adjustment. Even the approach to school change can be considered similar to the artistic process. Any theatrical production process begins with pre-planning as the director (school leader) creates a vision for the production. In this same way, a school leader holds a vision for the school environment and outcomes they aim to achieve. To execute that vision, the director then enlists the knowledge and help of the designers and creatives to implement it.

Throughout the rehearsal process, actors take risks to make a choice and try something. There is constant reflection and adjustments made through the process of rehearsal notes. This creative cycle process is identical to a cycle of improvement one may embark on as they move to make changes in their school. This section will review several organizational change models and how the Immersive Arts Integration model fits into their guiding principles.

McKinsey's 7S framework outlines the following seven strategies to consider when planning for change: 1) Strategy, 2) Structure, 3) Systems, 4) Shared Values, 5) Style, 6) Staff, and 7) Skills. Most schools have systems, structures, and styles in place. If considering a significant shift from a traditional to an Immersive Arts Integration approach, the leadership team more likely needs to explore the shared values, staff, and skills. In terms of shared values, here are some questions to consider:

- Does everyone on staff want to be part of an Immersive Arts Integration School?
- Do they value the arts as a means to an educational end?
- Does the school community value the arts and want their children to receive this type of education?

Staff should be considered in terms of their willingness to participate in the shift, what they may be able to contribute to the process, and at which stage. Who will be promoting the shift? Who will be resistant to the change because it is not a good match for them? The skill set of the staff is an important factor in terms of both their prerequisite knowledge or lack thereof and their willingness and capacity to learn new skills. There are several possible staff scenarios:

- Those who have an arts base and are willing to incorporate it
- Those who have an arts base and are unwilling to incorporate it
- Those who have no arts base and are willing to learn
- Those who have no arts base and are unwilling to learn

(McKinsey, 2012)

Recognizing all of these factors will inform any updates to the strategy, structure, and systems put in place to adopt an Immersive Arts Integration approach.

After studying over 700 organizations, Jeffrey Hiatt developed The ADKAR Model. The acronym stands for 1) Awareness (of the need to change), 2) Desire (to participate in and support the change), 3) Knowledge (on how to change), 4) Ability (to implement required skills and behaviors), and 5) Reinforcement (to sustain the change). The elements are not listed in sequential order, so they may be prioritized based on the composition of the school community. When applied to a school, the elements focus on the faculty and staff making the transition. When people's place in the process is considered, any resistance can be planned for and avoided which will ultimately result in a faster implementation. The key takeaway of this model is that instead of starting with change mandates, a conversation about the need for change happens first. Inclusion of and focus on people provides them with the confidence they need to complete the transformation. Because schools are such highly contextualized organizations, there are benefits to focusing on the people who will do the work (Hiatt, 2006).

John Kotter is another organizational change researcher and leader. He developed the 8 Step Process to Accelerate Change.

He outlines the following accelerators to implement change: 1) Create a sense of urgency, 2) Build a coalition, 3) Form a strategic vision and initiatives, 4) Enlist a volunteer army, 5) Enable action by removing barriers, 6) Generate short term wins, 7) Sustain acceleration, and 8) Institute change. As it relates to Immersive Arts Integration, someone must establish a sense of urgency. It could be the principal, superintendent, board of education, community, or parents; someone has to name and commit to being an arts school. The coalition will likely be people who have an arts background but could and should also include those who do not but are committed to the work. On a side note, throughout the book, the term "the leadership" is used. This intentionally references the cadre of people identified to lead the change; this is the volunteer army. The typical perceived barriers will include budget, schedule, and buy-in. These will need workarounds in the early planning stages so the shift can move forward on pace. The short-term wins will need to be coupled with the establishment of a trusting environment and permission for teachers to fail as they experiment. The leadership needs to acknowledge and reward early efforts to incorporate theatre strategies; since mini celebrations of work are incorporated in the planning approximately every six weeks, these present a great opportunity. The sustained acceleration and instituted change are necessary components of the Immersive Arts Integration model. Because the approach to this work is collaborative, the sustained acceleration and instituted change elements will be a continual source of focus for the school. Articulated cycles of reflection and revision will be built in the process to support the work's evolution (Kotter, 1996).

Leadership Theory

How to Lead the Change

Beyond the theories of organizational change in and of themselves, it is important to consider the type of school leader that best serves this model as well. McGregor's work describes two types of leaders: authoritarian (Theory X) and participative (Theory Y).

Authoritarian leaders assume their employees dislike work, need constant direction and supervision, and require rewards to achieve goals. Participative leaders assume their employees are self-motivated, seek and accept responsibility, and are involved in decision making and problem solving. Because of the nature of this work, which challenges teachers new to theatre to learn and use theatre strategies with no prior experience, it is strongly recommended that leaders adopt a participative approach with faculty (McGregor, 1960).

Similarly, Social Psychologist Kurt Lewin identified three styles of leadership: Autocratic (authoritarian), Democratic (participative), and Laissez Faire (delegative). Autocratic leadership is where leaders have complete power over their people. The leader makes all of the decisions, and the followers are expected to follow orders and execute them without question. This style of leadership should only be used when dealing with inexperienced employees or in crisis situations, as the lack of input and autonomy can have a negative impact on employee motivation over the longer term. Typically, this leadership style is unnecessary in school settings, but there may be cause to consider the approach if there are staff who actively try to sabotage the transition. Democratic (or participative) leadership is where the leader involves followers in the decision making process. Often, the leader may still make the final decision, but input from group members is encouraged in order to reach a decision. According to Lewin's research, this style is the most effective for group performance across the board. However, democratic decision making can be a slow process, so it may not be optimal in a time-critical situation. This leadership style is useful to help novice staff feel successful and vested in the transition and development process.

Laissez faire leadership is a hands-off approach where leaders delegate decision making authority to their followers and allow them to work largely on their own. This style should only be used with highly skilled and highly motivated employees who are capable of planning, making decisions, solving problems, and getting the job done without management intervention. If your school already has a focus on the arts, the staff may be able to manage minor shifts in the existing model. High levels of autonomy can be very motivating for those who are skilled and motivated enough to handle it, but it can have a negative impact on performance for those who need strong direction and guidance. Skilled leaders will know which approach to use, when to use it, and with whom to use it.

Ready to Launch

Model Overview
Now that you understand some of the theory and foundation for the work, it's time to jump into the model. The remaining chapters will walk you through the five tenets of the model. You'll learn the nuts and bolts of how to use the tenets to build out a sustainable model for your school successfully. The tenets are not intended to be followed in a linear fashion; rather, the leadership will need to make decisions regarding rollout based on the individual school needs and characteristics.

Tenet #1: Building Ensemble
Building Ensemble is the process of getting to know your peers (adult to adult, student to student, and adult to student) on a personal level. Ensemble is developed within the adult professional learning community, the classroom community, and the school community.

Daily time is allocated for Building Ensemble, but it also becomes the approach used by the school for all interactions. It intentionally creates an element of vulnerability and equalizes the power structure among all participants.

Tenet #2: Arts Integration into Core Content Instruction
The most essential component of the Immersive Arts Integration model is the integration of theatre strategies into the core content instruction. This requires a teacher's knowledge of core content and theatre strategies and the ability to bridge the two by planning a standards-based lesson complete with all components. If this is a shift for the school, well-articulated

professional development and cycles of support are provided until the practice is embedded.

Tenet #3: Creating Integrated Units of Study
This collaborative process joins core content teachers and arts specialists. Teachers identify key curriculum ideas of the content areas, while arts specialists identify authentic opportunities to infuse the arts. Teacher teams follow an eight-step protocol to find areas of overlap and map out the teaching and learning process. This approach results in more efficient teaching and allows students to make deeper connections by making cross curricular associations.

Tenet #4: Elevating the Role of the Arts Educators
Arts educators continue to serve in their traditional role as skill-based instructors. A true arts approach covers all five art forms: music (instrumental and choral), visual art, media, theatre, and dance. In addition, arts teachers are elevated to the role of co-planner, co-teacher, and resource for the school community. They serve as resources for the common goal of arts integration. This work requires specific professional development to both empower and prepare teachers for this new role.

Tenet #5: Spaces and Places
Art permeates all spaces throughout the school campus. It happens from curb to curb so that both inside and outside the school, it is visually and auditorily apparent that art is part of the educational process. Environments are created so that the immersive experience is possible. Performance becomes part of the daily experience.

Enjoy your journey!

2

Foundational Work

> When it was first introduced to me, it was scary. It definitely was something different, and it made me feel very nervous because I feel like I'm not so strong in those types of activities. But I think . . . all the faculty meetings and "the arts integration coach" and professional developments and teachers coming into our classes . . . made me feel more comfortable. **3rd Grade Teacher**

Now that you understand the theory behind the Immersive Arts Integration model, you are ready to begin building a foundation for success. Think of this chapter like stocking your pantry before winter. You'll read about key moves that will make the process and program fly.

In Chapter 1, we outlined the five major components of the model for you. Here they are again:

1. Ensemble Building
2. Arts Integration into Core Content Instruction
3. Integrated Units of Study
4. Elevating the Role of the Arts Teachers
5. Spaces and Places

Anyone who has tried to implement change in an educational environment knows that the work must begin, at minimum, one year prior to the teachers and students engaging in the learning. The buy-in, the commitment, the confidence of the educators, the involvement of the school community, and the district leadership support are keys to the ultimate and quick success of implementation. Unfortunately, sometimes educational programs are selected, teachers are allotted a few hours of professional development in the few days before the school year begins, and then administrators and district leadership are puzzled as to why the students are not connecting to the curriculum or model. Energy is then spent during the first year supporting teachers on the issues they are facing AFTER the initial classroom implementation, and students are trying to "catch up." If the model was presented initially in a timely fashion and teachers were able to feel comfortable with the approach, ask questions, fail, and learn themselves before getting in front of their students, much of the urgency spent "catching kids up" would be mitigated.

Having said this, as you read through the model, be sure you identify the work your school needs to do in preparation. All schools will be different. Part of this work will be to ensure commitment comes from the entire school community.

Who's In?

Identifying the Drivers and Supporters of the Work

The bottom line is that a group of people need to want to do this work. The work is **driven** by two main groups: school leadership and teachers. School leadership is going to establish the foundation, evaluate and adjust, and facilitate professional learning and implementation. The teachers are going to adapt their pedagogy as a result of professional learning, collaborate with colleagues, and make the work come alive for students. Teachers are the ones who will take the risks, fail, then persevere and evolve. The curriculum will not change, but the pedagogy will. It will probably be messy, but it will be worth it.

The work is **supported** by two main groups: the district leadership and the parents. The district leadership is the gatekeeper through which all programmatic change is launched. If they happen to be the drivers, great. If not, they'll need to be educated on this "arts thing" and commit at least conceptually and ideally commit financially also. Parent groups will need to be educated and routinely updated as well. Budget and belief systems dictate whether sports, arts, or both are part of curriculum, after school programming, or not at all. Knowing where the balance lies in your school community will help you navigate how to leverage your parent conversations.

Depending on the circumstance, the shift to immersive arts can be "top down" or "bottom up." In a "top down" scenario, the school community is told they are shifting to the model. This approach might be necessary to remedy enrollment discrepancies or to accommodate a district that is shifting to choice-based programs. In a "bottom up" scenario, the school community identifies the need and desire for the shift. This is the more desirable of the two options because there is likely to be more buy-in from all stakeholders.

The school team (ideally composed of leadership, teachers, and parents) will start with a general commitment to a shift to an Immersive Arts Integration approach. That process takes between six months and one year. Then, the school team will develop clarity about the specific artistic aspects and processes included in the program. That process will happen over time as staff receive professional development and the school community's strengths, weaknesses, and preferences become more evident. That process takes between one and two years.

Family Involvement

Engaging Community Support

There will likely come a time when it becomes important to educate and solicit feedback from families in the event there is an opportunity for them to move in or out of the school. It is beneficial to understand in what ways families support the model and where there are additional opportunities for further explanation. Opinions should be solicited through surveys and focus groups. Asking the right questions can provide leadership with valuable information regarding what they do and do not understand in order to determine the next steps in the process. See Appendix for sample parent survey.

The model is contingent upon the use of theatre strategies in the core curriculum, but there are other options in terms of skills-based arts instruction that will be of interest to parents. For example, schools can consider including the following:

- Offering strings or band instruction if it is not currently provided
- Extending strings or band instruction to other grades
- Offering world drumming, ceramics, dance, or other specialized visual or performing arts instruction

If there will be a shift in skills-based arts instruction, that information should be presented to parents. Some parents will support the shift, and some will not. In one example, several parents did not support dance as an option for their boys. They believed boys only needed physical education classes and would not want to dance. This presented an opportunity to educate families on the variety of dance genres; explore gender biases related to arts; present popular culture examples of successful boys and men who dance; and clarify student access to local and state physical education standards that could be met in a variety of ways.

Student Involvement

Identifying the Participants

Just like with staff, some students and their families may or may not be interested in an Immersive Arts Integration approach, and that's okay. If you're working in a large district that aims to offer a variety of choice programs, there are several ways to manage the shift in terms of student population.

- One option is to dismantle the current neighborhood school enrollment and rebrand it as a magnet or choice program. In this approach, all students would need to apply and then be enrolled through a lottery process. This may be desirable in scenarios where redistricting

is a consideration or where all schools in the district are shifting to a theme.
- ♦ A second option is to maintain the current neighborhood school enrollment and offer open seats in the Immersive Arts Integration school and seats in the surrounding schools so that students may transfer in or out. This allows families with strong connections to the neighborhood school to remain. Transportation is a consideration in this scenario. For public schools, state law will determine whether transportation must be provided to all students. If they are shifting to different schools, bus routes need to be adjusted and updated.
- ♦ A third option is to maintain the current neighborhood school enrollment and not offer seats in surrounding schools. This may be the only option for private schools or those in small districts. The information gathered in the surveys and focus groups will shed light on whether this is a viable option.

Staff Involvement

Navigating Backgrounds and Gauging Interest

It is also important to ensure that all staff are willing to participate in the transition. Some staff may not be interested in this instructional approach, and that's okay. If you're in a district with multiple elementary or middle schools, it provides the opportunity to identify staff from other schools who are very enthusiastic about the model and would like to participate or current staff who are not interested in the model and would like to transition to another school within the district.

It is critical the building leader has a clear understanding of the general education classroom teachers who will be doing the bulk of this work. Two key personnel factors will be their existing skill set and their willingness to participate. Three possible scenarios include the following:

- ♦ Teachers who have skills and knowledge and are willing to learn and implement theatre strategies

- Teachers who have no skills or knowledge and are willing to learn
- Teachers who have no skills or knowledge and are unwilling to learn and implement

The number of teachers in each listed category will determine the amount of time and effort the leader devotes to preparing the school community for the shift.

If your school is one already designated as an arts school or has in which the majority of teachers are knowledgeable about and willing to learn and implement, the leader will spend less time preparing for the work. There is no need to "sell" the model because the level of interest is already there. However, if "art" existed only in non-classroom spaces or if the only way art was integrated into the general education classroom was when arts teachers entered the general education classroom space, this would be a shift in practice.

If your school is a traditional school looking to make a shift and is composed predominantly of teachers who are willing to make the shift, the management considerations will pertain to creating an environment ripe for risk taking, acceptance of failure, relying on peer support to tackle challenging instructional strategies, and developing systems of coaching cycles. Once teachers understand they have a safe space in which to experiment and master the new pedagogical techniques, the progress will move forward more quickly. Because these strategies are not taught in teacher preparation classes, most teachers will have no experience in using them, barring a background in theatre. Understanding this will make the work happen more organically.

There will be some circumstances where a portion of the faculty will not be knowledgeable about or willing to learn about and implement the four theatre strategies. It may be that the district has designated a particular school to make a shift to the arts and that the critical mass of teachers did not want and are not receptive to the shift. It may be that the school leader has identified the transition to the arts, but the critical mass of teachers is not on board. Or it may be that a portion of the staff is open and a portion of the staff is not. In these circumstances, all decisions and actions must originate from the school's designation as an arts school. Once that happens, a promise is made to the school community about a deliverable set of outcomes that will define the school experience for students. As soon as that mission and vision is clearly identified, every action step becomes about living up to that promise. So, a teacher may choose not to teach core content with theatre strategies, but they will not be meeting the parent, community, and student expectations. This type of pressure typically results in teachers coming on board or moving on to a different school.

Once the professional development around the four theatre strategies is taught and internalized, it is important to consider how incoming teachers are inculcated into the system. Because the model weighs so heavily on peer coaching and planning, it is an easy lift to onboard new teachers or those changing grade levels. This is an improvement over curriculum strategies that are constantly shifting because veteran teachers and students bring new teachers up to speed quickly. The same is to be said for new students joining the school. The student's knowledge of a strategy needed to be one that if a new student entered third grade that they, too, with time and practice, could easily assimilate the strategies into their learning.

What do we do with the teachers with no background that we are asking to do this work? Those teachers are either open to the idea or not. For those open to the idea, they need to develop the ability to feel comfortable lying on the floor like an octopus and walking around the library as if they were in mud. For those not open to the idea, it's up to the administrator to connect the teacher to the work. For example, a baseball coach who has found himself teaching in a seventh-grade Immersive Arts Integration math class can connect to the work by bringing baseball into his teaching practice. It might take some coaxing for him to see the vision, but showing him the path and making those initial connections for him will lead to a faster adoption of the process.

Once the context of those doing the work is clear and you've identified who will be doing it, the playing field is level. You are in a prime position to onboard everyone at the same time. There are times when new programs or approaches are piloted in one grade level or with a subgroup of staff; this is not recommended. Because the learning will likely be new for many people, there is a unique opportunity for everyone to learn together, fail together, laugh together, and evolve together. This will happen quickly and organically as teacher teams co-plan units of study and lessons. You'll read more about this in Chapters 4 and 5. Through this process, the staff will become very connected and supportive of each other.

Budget

Who's Paying for All of This?

Funding may be needed to address staffing, programming, materials, and capital projects. Here are some considerations:

- ♦ A staff member is needed to provide ongoing professional development for teachers and current skill-based arts teachers (i.e., Art and Music teachers). The professional development model (discussed in subsequent chapters) combines the facilitation of workshop-style teacher training, job-imbedded coaching cycles, and co-planning with classroom teachers and skill-based arts teachers. Because the professional development is so comprehensive, it is strongly suggested that an Arts Integration Specialist or Coach is hired. In this role, the staff member could provide professional development in addition to skill-based theatre instruction for students.
- ♦ Additional skill-based staff may be considered, such as a Theatre Teacher, Dance Teacher, and/or Music Teacher if they are not already part of the faculty. These could be full or part time positions.
- ♦ Additional arts programming could be considered. For example, the school may want to design, create, and install a mural that would require hiring a local artist for a one-time fee. Or perhaps there are additional enrichment programs from traveling theatre companies that would present and serve as a model for student productions for a one-time fee.

- There will be associated materials costs for any additional skill-based arts programs such as dance costumes, microphones, or paint.
- Capital projects should be considered as well. Perhaps a classroom space needs to be converted to a dance studio, or furniture needs to be purchased for a strings ensemble. Capital projects are typically funded by the city or have a separate line item in a district budget.

The development of a self-sustaining program requires a financial commitment by the district or school and the school community. At the bare minimum, an Arts Integration Coach or Teacher needs to be hired and assumed as an ongoing operating cost for the model. The other items mentioned can be allocated on a part time or yearly basis.

As with any other initiative, funding can be provided from the district, state magnet school funding, grants, or fundraising. Arts grants abound. The Arts Integration Coach or Specialist can lead the grant-writing effort with support from staff or families. Fundraising will also inherently become part of the process. Committed parent groups can generate funds via the typical baked goods sales and auctions. Consider pairing the outcome with the ask – auction a collective piece of student artwork to raise funds for a future mural project or auction music lessons to support the purchase of new instruments. It will be important to identify funding sources that are sustainable over time so that the key components of the educational program become guaranteed experiences for the school community.

Communication Plan

Shout It from the Rooftops!
From inception to full implementation, the transition to an Immersive Arts Integration model should include frequent and transparent communication with the school community. This will build trust and enthusiasm for the shift. In the early stages of the process, you will want to communicate information regarding any teacher interest surveys, parent forums, or community

questionnaires. As often as possible, include direct quotes from participants; these will provide context for the numbers.

Once you have established an arts focus, load your website and social media platforms with clips of teacher professional development. Families want to see staff enjoying themselves as they learn new skills. Highlight student artwork and collaboration. So often, arts are thought of in terms of the big production at the end. While this is enjoyable, it's more about the process through which students are learning than about the product. Be sure to highlight the process. Pre-existing regular communication should be adapted to include messaging about the arts. Consider ways you may wish to communicate student mastery of new arts skills. If you add a theatre or dance class, how will you let parents know how their child is doing in those classes? The team may wish to consider a progress report to accompany prior formal standard academic report cards. You'll read more about this in Chapters 4 and 5 and find a sample progress report in the Appendix.

Implementation Steps and Timeline

How Long Is This Going to Take?

The goal of the Immersive Arts Integration model is to transform a school from a baseline to a self-sustaining stage within four years. The timeline will vary greatly depending on the needs of

TABLE 2.1 Implementation Steps by Year

Year	Task	Steps
1	Foundational Work	Identify Model Staff and Family Presentation Identify Staff In/Out Identify Students In/Out Shared PD Experience
2	Partial Implementation	Teachers Learn Strategies Teachers and Arts Teachers co-plan three key units of study
3	Full Implementation	Teachers Use Strategies Teachers and Arts Teachers co-plan three additional units of study
4	Refinement	Teachers Learn Advanced Strategies

individual schools. If the school has not previously had an arts focus and all staff will need to be trained, it will take the full amount of time. If the concept is familiar and the right people are in the right positions, it can be expedited. Table 2.1 includes broad steps for implementing the process.

Professional Development Timeline

Transforming Staff from Novice to Practicing

The key to successful implementation is constant and consistent professional development. We have all been part of scenarios where school systems buy into a curriculum, provide one or two professional development opportunities, and then expect full implementation. As soon as district schedules, competing priorities, or contract restrictions on teachers arise, the initiative fails. Because the Immersive Arts Integration model is crafted with a combination of professional development, adult cooperative learning, and the co-creation of resources, it becomes part of the school's fabric and will be sustained through a variety of changes.

Classroom teachers will need professional development to learn the four theatre strategies and how to implement them in their classrooms. Arts teachers will need to learn how to co-plan units of study. Administrators will need to learn how to schedule for collaboration and professional development; how to set expectations for look-fors; and if and how to evaluate the new pedagogical style. The following table includes the broad steps for teacher professional development that will launch the summer before Year 2.

Decisions will need to be made regarding who and how the professional development and calibration will take place. The school needs to identify who will be providing the professional development. Listed in the following are options ranging from most to least ideal and most to least costly:

- ♦ Hire a 1.0 full time equivalent Arts Integration Specialist to focus solely on coaching staff and running co-planning sessions

TABLE 2.2 Professional Development Timeline

Session Number	Professional Development Session	Suggested Time
PD 1	Foundations of the Work/Setting Up Space	Summer Prior to starting the work
PD 2	Shared Artistic Experience	August
PD 3	Shared Arts Education Experience	September
PD 4	Ensemble Building	September
PD 5	Tableaux	October
PD 6	Pantomime	November
PD 7	Walking in Space	December
PD 8	Improvisation	January
PD 9	Building Integrated Lesson Plans	February
PD 10	Creating Integrated Units of Study	March

- Hire one person to serve as a .5 Arts Integration Specialist and a .5 Theatre teacher
- Hire a consultant to instruct staff on theatre strategies on a weekly or monthly basis
- Hire a consultant to instruct staff on theatre strategies on a quarterly basis

There are times when staff will need to learn and practice the theatre strategies and co-planning process. This will take place when students are not in session. Opportunities may include the following:

- Faculty meetings
- Early release days
- Summer workshops
- Vacation workshops
- Release time during school days

There are times when staff will need to practice using the theatre strategies and watching one another use them. This will take place in class with students' debriefing sessions either before or after each session. Leadership should intentionally plan to be a part of or not be a part of this process. This will depend on the level of comfort staff has with being vulnerable and taking risks in front of colleagues. Opportunities may include the following:

- Arts Integration Specialist or Coach models in class with students
- Classroom teacher models for the Arts Integration Specialist or Coach
- Grade level teachers participate in coaching cycles:
  - Week 1: Coach and Teachers A/B/C co-plan a lesson. Coach models in Class A, Teachers A/B/C watch, then debrief
  - Week 2: Coach and Teachers A/B/C co-plan a lesson. Teacher A models in Class A, Coach and Teachers B/C watch, then debrief
  - Week 3: Coach and Teachers A/B/C co-plan a lesson. Teacher B models in Class B; Coach and Teachers A/C watch, then debrief
  - Week 4: Coach and Teachers A/B/C co-plan a lesson. Teacher C models in Class C; Coach and Teachers A/B watch, then debrief

In subsequent coaching cycles, teachers can plan independently and then participate in the observations. Teachers can also teach in homerooms other than their own. Teachers can lead this process in schools that do not employ a coach or consultant.

It is important that school administrators assign value to the work by observing the planning and practice of the theatre strategies in class, providing feedback, and potentially evaluating. It is important to note that the observations take place around the instruction and do not necessarily focus on the performances. Opportunities may include the following:

- Lesson and/or unit plan reviews to ensure the theatre strategies are incorporated
- Observation of the coaching cycles
- Informal walkthroughs and associated feedback
- Formal evaluation process

It is strongly recommended that administrators identify their expectations prior to observing and providing feedback in order to be transparent and build trust. Especially during early implementation, this is not a "gotcha" game but rather an effort to consistently applaud efforts by staff to evolve.

Now that you have identified the who and the when, what happens next?

Arts Is a Yes! Now What?

Empowering Teachers to Shape the Future of Their School

It's time to create some buzz with staff. For the first post-commitment professional development opportunity, consider taking staff to a local museum, theatre performance, or concert. Steep yourselves in an inspirational artistic experience. You want to level the playing field and provide a shared experience that you can refer back to when talking about this work. If you have staff that wants to do the work but has no background in the arts, this will give them a launching pad and mental framework. When you design the offsite experience, make sure you craft it with the intent to inspire everyone to be connected with a way of thinking and feeling about art. School staff almost always have dry professional development experiences inside their schools. Taking them offsite will validate them as professionals and create energy around the new work. Here are some ideas for this launch:

- Go to a musical performance. Before the visit, study the composer, musicians, and context around the work. After the performance, share your opinions of it. Talk about whether the audience was engaged or not and why.
- See a play or musical. Before the visit, study the playwright, the theme, and the context of the work. After the performance, share your opinions of it. Talk about the role of the audience.
- Visit a museum. Before the visit, study the type of artist. Draw from that experience the takeaways you want your students to have.

Another key step to engage staff is to task them with researching other schools that are doing the same type of work. This will inspire them to dream big about your school. What can you glean from other schools' websites? Look for course offerings, performances, etc., that you would like included in your model. Schedule site visits with groups of teachers. Visit arts themed schools either in person or virtually. Go prepared with a list of questions. Go with an open mind. Internalize components of other programs that would make sense for your school.

Make a dream board and have staff contribute ideas. Don't give voice to constraints (budget, schedule, facilities). Dream Big. You will start to build a vision of the school in which you all want to teach and learn. Conversations like these tend to go one of two ways: either there is a focus on large scale productions and experiences that are unattainable without a serious financial commitment, or there is an inability to think beyond what the school already offers. Encourage staff to incorporate both. A key to the success of this work is that **EVERYONE is INVOLVED from the beginning,** so be sure to celebrate that involvement!

How the Integration Happens

Fitting the Integration Throughout the Day
The Immersive Arts Integration model is best suited for elementary and middle schools, but there may be different considerations based on their structures.

Elementary
In an Immersive Arts Instruction school, it's about three things: teaching core content with theatre strategies, integrating the arts forms with core content, and using the artistic process as a vehicle through which learning happens. In most elementary schools, there is one general education teacher and separate related arts teachers. Since the general education teacher leads most of the academic activities throughout the day, that teacher controls the amount of time dedicated to all subjects versus the combination of subjects. The classroom teacher, therefore, can

determine which subjects are taught with theatre strategies and which are not. This makes planning and co-planning relatively straightforward.

Middle

In a secondary school, there are multiple teachers in charge of core content. Integrating with one another and then integrating with related arts requires a level of flexibility in terms of planning and scheduling. The master schedule must be created such that a social studies and reading teacher can combine periods to co-teach a unit that might require content knowledge regarding a particular war paired with a novel about the same war. In a larger middle school, it might be helpful to subdivide the school into a section that utilizes Immersive Arts Integration. Then, a smaller subset of teachers would need to coordinate schedules and planning time.

Now that you have established a solid foundation and plan for the work, it's time to get started!

3

Ensemble Building

> It was the teachers that made it successful. Everybody has a buy-in. To my knowledge, there weren't really too many people who were skeptical of it and said, "Okay, I don't want to do it." . . . Nobody transferred or left because this program was starting. **Arts Integration Specialist**

Okay. Now it's time to get to work. You've engaged the stakeholders; everyone is excited; families see and understand the value of this approach on their students' learning; the teachers feel grounded in the approaches and confident to try with students; and staff are engaged in the process and support all the "extra" ways the school is immersing in the work.

The first tenet of the Immersive Arts Integration model is Ensemble Building. It is the process of getting to know your peers (adult to adult, student to student, and adult to student) on a personal level. Ensemble is developed within the adult professional learning community, the classroom community, and the school community. Daily time is allocated for the Ensemble Building. In all its forms, no one person holds more power than another, and all are valued equally. This tenet contributes or sets the stage (pardon the pun) for a healthy climate and for social emotional learning.

This chapter will start by focusing on ensemble at the student level, then the adult level, then the community level. It is important to note that the term ensemble refers to both a <u>group of people</u> and a <u>process of connecting.</u>

Bridging Ensemble from Theatre to Schools

What's the Connection?

If you are approaching this work with little theatre experience, you know the value and importance of having a strong ensemble. If this concept is new to you, let's take a moment to articulate that process. In the theatrical process, a creative may be asked to be vulnerable to perform a character that has to tap into deep sadness or darkness. They may also be asked to take great risks to perform as a clown or in a farcical way. Creating a space where actors feel safe to be vulnerable and brave to take risks has always been inherent in the theatre process. The idea is that everyone feels equally creative and valued. Ensemble is created in large and small ways – hosting all cast and crew dinners, starting all rehearsals in a circle and breathing collectively together, or learning about each other in more personal ways.

In the theatrical process, each rehearsal begins in a circle, and actors engage in a physical and vocal warm up. This allows the actor to empty their mind and body of the daily stresses and to open themselves up to receive the lessons of the rehearsal. The power of the circle also indicates that no one person is more important than another. While the director is there to moderate and guide, the rehearsal circle is the space owned by all who inhabit it.

Building on this foundation of ensemble, respect, and trust, actors engage in the process of repetitious risk taking. Each rehearsal has a structure of knowing which pages in the script are to be rehearsed, but the journey to get there is individualized, and the director will allow time and space for the actors to make their own meaning of the text. Sometimes, there are very concrete goals and objectives that must be met – an actor must make it downstage center to hit a light cue or to be out of the way to move a set piece, but the rest of the journey is exploratory.

By now, hopefully, you are seeing the inherent connections and value of building an ensemble in the theatre and building an ensemble in your classroom. But to be certain, let's walk through it together.

Students are often asked to be vulnerable and share an answer in class or be brave and stand in front of the room to present a project. For some students, this is a terrifying task – typically because they are afraid of being teased. They are afraid to make a mistake and not have the support of their classmates when they do. In the Immersive Arts Integration classroom, it is part of the students' process to take a risk and fail in the comfort that their ensemble will be there to support them AND celebrate their efforts.

Building Ensemble with Students

Everyone Is a Star Because No One Is a Star

Building an ensemble and creating a classroom that is both safe and brave is different than and more involved than asking getting-to-know-you questions on the first few days of school. It is a culture shift in individual classrooms that, in time, manifests itself into the school culture. This classroom culture of community can be hard to come by in contemporary classrooms. Teachers are often lamenting that they just do not have time to cover all the content. The reasons range from needing to teach pre-content that they had not anticipated (students are not coming to the next grade level prepared) to students sharing they do not have time to do all the homework and classwork that is required of them. Students also long for work that feels authentic to their futures and that they see as having applicable value.

Ensemble directly translates to "together" in French. Ensembles exist in performing arts but also in other areas of life where people work together. When you first come together as an ensemble, challenge students to think about other areas of life where ensembles exist (sports teams, clubs, etc.). In Chapter 7, Spaces and Places, you'll identify <u>where</u> and <u>how</u> the ensemble will take place. For now, we'll talk about <u>what</u> you'll be doing to support the tenet. Start by getting students together in a circle. Be explicit – explain that it helps to get to know one another on a deeper level if everyone cares about one another and wants to do their best work for each other. When people make personal connections, they are more likely to form friendships and alliances.

The ensemble is a way of standing and a place in the room where stuff happens, but it also describes a way of participating with one another, specifically to prime expression and connectivity. During the ensemble in an educational setting, theatre activities are used to establish rapport and connectedness and later for processing content and curriculum. Ensemble activities can start quite simply and then evolve to include complex instructions and content-related vocabulary.

It is important to note that asking students to stand in a circle may be a new endeavor. Not all schools or classrooms have asked this of students before. Students have been conditioned to attend school by sitting at a desk, so there will be a variety of reactions to getting together depending on students' ages. Reactions may range from giddy five-year-olds to sullen middle schoolers. As you would with any other routine, expectations should be established. Remind students to be aware of their space relative to their peers. Until the process becomes a norm, it is okay to put dots or tape on the floor to indicate their spots in the circle. The tried and true technique of having students get into a circle with their arms out to be sure enough space is between everyone always works. There will also be times when ensemble activities will involve physical contact. Depending on everyone's comfort levels, these activities may take more time to ease into. It's not okay to bump into a friend while walking around the room, and they may be inclined to, so please remember that, like with anything, getting students moving about the room and into nontraditional classroom formations will take time. Part of ensemble building is the norming of ensemble activities. There will be a continuum of comfort for teachers (and students, for that matter) in playing theatre games in classrooms. Some will be comfortable with trying out something new. Others might be intimidated by chaotic energy. When developing ensembles, it is important to establish parameters around behavior. Another great tip is to establish with students early the concept of "actor neutral," which is when students return their model to a still position – often with their arms down by their sides and silent. If energy starts to skew, the teacher can always call "actor neutral," and students should return to the neutral stance.

Teachers should take time to modify activities for their students but not lose sight of the goal of putting them in a circle and having them share their personal thoughts and reflections in the space. Administrators should also be reminded that organized chaos and allowing time for students to acclimate to it is part of the onboarding of this process of implementing Immersive Arts Integration.

Ensemble in the Classroom

Traditional Morning Meeting Versus Ensemble

When groups of people gather over time or in a place within a classroom or learning space, there is a process of connection that unfolds. At times, the connection is healthy, and individuals contribute to the give and take of the learning process. At times, the connection is unhealthy; there may be a class clown, a bully, or one who monopolizes the air time. When there is intentional planning for an ensemble with established ground rules for how people treat one another, it creates a condition within which students can evolve as a cohort in structured and unstructured parts of the day.

In a traditional classroom, students enter the classroom, put away belongings, have a choice of activities to engage in, then sit at their seats, listen to the morning announcements, and then the formal morning meeting is launched. Students often are moved to a carpet and again sit in rows with their attention on their teacher, who is often sitting in a chair above them. Teachers will often start a morning meeting with a question for the students: "What did you do this weekend?" "What are you looking forward to over winter break?" or perhaps more school related, "What is a goal for your week?" Students are often asked to raise their hands, and those who wish to share are allowed to. Sometimes, all students must respond, and, in some cases, there is only time for a few students to respond. In those situations, a few unintended consequences may arise:

1. Students who did not have anything fun to share over the weekend do not speak
2. The same students share each day
3. A climate of competition may be created if students try to share what they perceive to be valued by their peers or society
4. A climate of cultural insensitivity may be fostered if there is a disparity between students' socioeconomic status

Of course, teachers do many things to manage the preceding trends: creating lists to make sure by the end of the week everyone speaks, creating a schedule so students know when it is their turn to share, or picking numbers so students are selected at random. The issue with these approaches is that it is a lot of extra work for the teacher, and while it archives the goal of students speaking, they are not speaking from an authentic or intrinsically motivated place. It is another assignment to complete.

In an Immersive Arts Integration classroom, the school day starts when students enter the classroom, manage their belongings, and engage in opening activities to connect with one another. This is a precious opportunity to inspire students for the day's learning and establish a safe space for risk taking and rewards. It is best practice for adults to be present at the door to greet students with a smile and kind words. After the morning's logistical tasks (attendance, lunch count, unpacking backpacks), it's time to launch the ensemble. This is a brand of morning meetings that includes theatre games as a way to connect the participants. Theatre games are different from ice breakers because students are often in roles during these games and/or are active using their bodies. It's important to use the term "ensemble" because it signals a concrete connection to the arts.

The ensemble meeting is different from the typical classroom morning meeting in several ways. Morning meetings are typically teacher-led and serve to complete daily tasks (attendance, lunch count, calendar, review expectations, preview academic learning) while perhaps having students share something about themselves. When executed poorly, there is a high risk for redundancy, cultural insensitivity if one tradition becomes the norm, and a space created for students to highlight their access to socioeconomic advantages over their peers (vacations or experiences when peers may not have the same access). Conversely, the purpose of building an ensemble is for the group to evolve collectively over time by increasing familiarity, trust, and acceptance.

First, both adults and students gather in a circle. A circle allows each member to be valued equally. Members can also see one another, and no one can hide or shrink away. Each person has someone on both sides, which creates a sense of trust and belonging. The circle can be in an open area of the room, within desks, or around desks, depending on the space restrictions. Then, each member of the circle gets in "actor neutral." This is a stance where feet are hip-width apart and arms are by the side. Hands are soft, and facial expressions are neutral. Gaze is softly forward. It is important to practice this stance so that students can return to it when they need to regroup. Once the neutral stance is established, theatre games can be introduced. The group plays a short game which is intended to celebrate the individual and the group. A list of sample games is included later in this chapter. The games should be simple and then develop in complexity over time and grade level. While the classroom teacher may need to teach the games in the beginning, the process should evolve so that it becomes student-led when appropriate.

Impact of Ensemble on Students

What's the Payoff?
Once ensemble is established as a daily practice in the classroom and school, there will be noticeable positive outcomes in terms of risk taking and climate. Because the ensemble activities are designed to result in a deeper understanding of the other person and to create a sense of unity in the space, there is a greater connection between people. Because some of the games are designed to target emotions, there is a greater awareness of emotional range and impact. This is useful on a variety of levels, including insight into one another and characters in a story.

Ensemble in the School

Setting the Tone for the School
In addition to the benefits of the ensemble start to the day there are also opportunities for Immersing the arts into the morning routines. Many schools begin their day with morning announcements over the loudspeaker that usually include the Pledge of Allegiance, a song, birthday acknowledgements, and any additional pertinent information. In Immersive Arts Instruction schools, announcements may also include a performance of some sort. This is a great way to include a piece of writing or music either as a culminating academic activity or creative endeavor. If announcements are done using live or recorded video, there is an additional opportunity to include a visual performance or element as well. It is important to use the term "ensemble" because it represents a specific and unique part of the school day.

Building Ensemble with Staff

Shared Arts Experiences to Create Connections
The adults in the school will also benefit from intentionally planned activities that serve to create a fun, engaging, and rigorous environment committed to offering exceptional learning experiences for students. Ensemble norms are established through shared experiences, professional development, meetings, and other formal and informal opportunities. If we want students to have a fun learning experience, we must make sure the adults do as well!

When working with groups of adults, you may want to consider factors similar to those impacting students. Be mindful that you are working to create an environment safe for risk taking and creativity that is safe for all voices, and consider the following:

- ♦ How do you ensure all voices are valued?
- ♦ Are there seating arrangements that would support equal participation from all?

- How do you ensure all staff participate?
- Are there cliques? Do they need to be broken or can you capitalize on their energy?
- How will you manage the adult who monopolizes the conversation and the one who is quiet in the corner?
- Provide space for socializing.

Knowing your audience will allow you to plan for a positive experience for all.

As we discussed in Chapter 2, as you launch the work, be sure to plan a fun, shared off site experience to the extent your budget allows. It is important for these experiences to be grounded in professional learning so that the teacher learns new instructional practices while modeling for them how to translate the work into the classroom effectively. It's fun to move outside the building, but make it count! These experiences can result in shifting disconnected teachers to ones who are now bound by a common experience and a common understanding of the work they are embarking on. If they come to the work with little or no arts background, their knowledge base about and appreciation for the arts will have evolved. The best part is they will be inspired to use intentional field trips for their students.

Ensemble in Professional Development

Learning, Owning, Expanding

Teacher professional development for this tenet is most effectively modeled and then supported by teachers co-creating and contributing to a shared body of strategies. Once the school has identified its path toward Immersive Arts Integration, the very first professional development opportunity, then at each and every professional development session thereafter (whether related to the arts or not), the collective group of adults should start in a circle in the ensemble. This will establish all participants as equal, encourage risk taking, eliminate cliques, and level the playing field so the work can begin.

In the first session, the concept of ensemble will be explicitly taught. Since adults learn at a faster pace than students, you may consider moving through the activities at a faster rate or starting with more complex activities. Since adults are often more guarded than children, it may take a few meetings before everyone is on board. Be patient. The boisterous and courageous staff will lead, but the rest will follow. If this is new territory for your school, it will be a drastic departure from the dry faculty meetings with leadership or presenter at the front and staff seated with varying degrees of attention. It is important to note that some more traditional meetings often begin with icebreakers. The purpose of the icebreaker, however, is for members to get to know one another. The purpose of an ensemble is to create a connectedness and a sense of unity. Icebreakers are often designed in pairs or small groups that may or may not return to the whole group. The ensemble always starts and finishes as a group. As you are building the model, it is imperative that early and strong bonds are created within the group and between the group and the work. Once established, these bonds will allow for the other tenets (especially using theatre strategies to teach core content as outlined in Chapter 4 and coaching cycles during which teachers observe one another teaching) to develop smoothly. It

TABLE 3.1 Professional Development Timeline

Session Number	Professional Development Session	Suggested Time
PD 1	Foundations of the Work/Setting Up Space	Summer Prior to starting the work
PD 2	Shared Artistic Experience	August
PD 3	Shared Arts Education Experience	September
PD 4	Ensemble Building	September
PD 5	Tableaux	October
PD 6	Pantomime	November
PD 7	Walking in Space	December
PD 8	Improvisation	January
PD 9	Building Integrated Lesson Plans	February
PD 10	Creating Integrated Units of Study	March

is recommended that between two and four ensemble games be presented and then repeated in the first few meetings so that staff truly know them inside and out. Once the staff is ready, they can lead the game at a session. Better yet, they can lead the game in their classrooms with students!

The ensemble games should be stored in a shared drive with all participants having editing rights. This will transition the ownership from the trainer or presenter to the staff. The next step is for staff to develop and upload their own games or variations of other games to the drive. Administrators should take note of any new games in the drive and create a space for the teacher to lead their game at a meeting. Also, be sure to create space for teachers to share how the ensemble games were received by students. Did they laugh? What did you do when they got too silly? What would you have done differently to make the game more meaningful? Teachers will want to hear about successes and mishaps from one another. It is important for teachers to build this early foundation for instructional and pedagogical risk taking so they can transfer that spirit to the other tenets of the model.

Lesson Planning

Be Intentional

Daily lesson plans are expected to include an ensemble game. Since it is not a core academic subject, plans can be very brief. They should all include an objective, the name of the game (the game instructions are located in your shared drive), and any other relevant notes. The objectives of the ensemble games will almost always be one of the following:

- ♦ Students will be able to express themselves verbally and physically
- ♦ Students will be able to develop social connections with other members of the classroom community

We'll talk more about lesson planning in Chapter 4.

Planning for Diverse Learners

Steps to Success

Ensemble games should be selected based on the learners in your space. It is imperative that all learners have access and are included. You may want to consider some of the following learner profiles and preparations:

- Are there any mobility considerations?
- Does my space allow for this game?
- How will I start and stop the game?
- What if students get too loud and silly?
- What if a student is not comfortable with this game?
- Will all the multilingual learners or students with disabilities have access?
- Do the games account for all students' cultural and ethnic backgrounds?

Some classes are sillier than others. Don't let that deter you! Find ways to harness the energy. You likely have already established a system of gathering student attention (call and repeat, peace sign, claps, etc.). If you have a rambunctious class, be sure to repeat your attention grabber prior to the ensemble game. Use proximity with a student who may get overstimulated. Select ensemble games that are less active or verbal in the beginning, then gradually include them. The ensemble games are such a fun part of the day that students will rise to the occasion.

Many ensemble games are nonverbal and, therefore, more easily accessed by multilingual learners or students with disabilities. As you increase the complexity, include visual supports or partner students with a peer who can guide them. You can also use proximity and model the game until the student is more independent. Theatre games sometimes involve physical contact – depending on students' individual comfort levels, we should always be mindful of everyone's personal bodies and space.

Some students will be uncomfortable with the ensemble in general, or they will be uncomfortable with a particular ensemble game. Maintaining a predictable daily routine is a key component to increasing their participation. Once they see the ensemble game played a few times and see their peers joining, they will be more apt to play. Having students in a circle will always give students a partner on both sides of them and eliminate the need for "selection" (which inherently includes the risk of someone not being selected). Finally, always give students the right to pass. Passing takes the pressure off and allows the student to stay in the circle but not participate at that particular moment. Use your best judgment on whether to return to them after their initial pass.

Assessment at the Classroom and School Levels

How Do You Know if Ensemble Is Working?

There are tangible and intangible results of building an ensemble. At the classroom level (or at the school level using aggregate scores), teachers could choose to measure participation rates, effort (though rather subjective), behavior referral rates, social emotional growth using a rating scale, or performance on the ensemble game (i.e., remembering every peer's name and adjective in a given game). At the school level, leadership could choose to measure the number of performances shared during announcements, the classroom participation rates via walkthroughs, the number of games included in the shared drive (for teachers), or the parent perception of school-home relationships based on a parent survey (for community). Observational data will also reveal the level of trust, risk taking, and mutual respect that results from an increased understanding of one another (adult to adult, student to student, and adult to student). Are people speaking kindly of one another? Do people give one another wait time when they're trying to answer a question? Are people laughing together? There is something to be said for the "feeling" you get when you enter a space. Trust it.

Teacher Supervision Versus Teacher Evaluation

Accountability Is Not a Scary Word

As you will see with each tenet of the Immersive Arts Integration model, there is a continuum of development and expectations. Ensemble Building is a relatively straightforward component that, once presented, can be implemented virtually immediately. The ultimate expectation after the first year is that ensemble takes place at the school level and classroom level daily each morning and includes an ensemble game that is led by a rotation of teachers and students, resulting in increased connectedness, mutual respect, and risk taking. As the teacher is learning the tenet, the frequency of implementation may be inconsistent.

Sample Ensemble Activities

What follows is a list of classic theatre games that are intended to be used during ensemble time at the beginning or end of the school day. Teachers will learn the games during their professional development opportunities before launching them to students. The games should be documented online so that all staff have access to them and can add to them. Remember that in the ensemble, all participants (adults included!) are in a circle. For simplicity's sake, we'll name the first participant P1, the second participant P2, and so on. Be mindful of your space, and be sure you account for anyone needing accommodations in the space. The person who knows the game should model it first to be sure everyone understands. Most games have a simple level and can become increasingly complex as needed. Remember to celebrate mistakes and mishaps–they are part of the journey! As students become more adept at the games, they can lead them and adapt them. The intended ages are listed, but feel free to adjust as needed. Have fun!

Call Back Techniques – *when you have the students in stations or small groups and it is getting loud and exciting, these are some techniques to help get them quiet and refocused*

It's important to know how to manage your group before you launch into the activity. In the beginning, students might be hesitant to participate and be vocal, but hopefully, that will be short lived, and they will be enthusiastic and committed! What follows are some options to recenter their focus after a high energy activity.

- If you hear my voice clap once/If you hear my voice clap twice
- Clap a pattern and have students repeat it back
- Create a call and response unique to your class (a lyric from a song – you say, "Hey," and they say something back). Another is you say, "A Hush . . ." and the class says, ". . . falls over the crowd."
- Call out "Actor Neutral" for students to stand still and quiet with eyes on the teacher
- Direct students to put their eyes on the ceiling, eyes on the door, eyes on me . . . .

Centering Activities

The following are two activities that are longer than call back techniques, shorter than games, and are designed to reduce the energy level slowly.

Pass the Object: As a follow-up to an active engagement, shift students to this pantomime activity where students sit in a circle on the rug, and you pass an imaginary object around the circle. For calming purposes, pass something light like a feather or delicate crystal.

Group Mirror: Have students sit in a circle, and the teacher first starts a slow motion (slow hand raises up, everyone follows, and etc. . . .). Once everyone is following, calm, and focused, you can ask another student to be the leader. The goal is for anyone to become a leader without any prompting.

Ensemble Games
Name Game (Grades K-8)

Level 1. Student A will say their name clearly and loudly. Student B (who is standing next to Student A on either side) will repeat the name of Student A, and then say their own name. Student C (who is standing two spaces past Student A and next to Student B) will repeat the names of Student A and Student B and then repeat their name. The game will carry on until all participants have said their names.

Level 2. Student A will say their name and add a gesture (such as a wave or head nod). Student B will repeat the name of Student A and their gesture, then say their own name and do their own gesture. Student C will repeat the names and gestures of Student A and Student B, then repeat their name. The game will carry on until all participants say their names and gestures.

Level 3. Student A will say their name and make their gesture. Student A will then "bounce" the turn to another player somewhere in the circle other than directly next to them. Turns will continue to bounce from player to player until all have participated.

Ball Toss (Grades K-8)

Level 1. Student A says their name. Then Student A says the name of Student B, and hands, rolls, or underhand throws the ball to them. Student B says their name and the name of P3, and hands, rolls, or underhand throws the ball to them.

Level 2. Participants can volunteer to say everyone's name in the circle.

Shark (Grades 2–5)

Students can ask each other for help to remember names.

Level 1. One student is a shark and stands in the middle of the ensemble circle and makes a chomping motion with their hands. The shark walks toward Student A (anywhere in the circle). Student A shouts the name of Student B (any other student in the circle). Student B must say the name of Student A before the shark reaches Student A. If the shark reaches Student A before they can exchange names with Student B, then the shark and Student A change spots, and Student A becomes the shark. If not, then the shark remains in the middle.

Level 2. Use first names in combination with middle and/or last names.

Level 3. Use a combination of names with a chosen gesture (see Name Game mentioned previously).

Stealing Spots (Grades 1–5)

This game adds lots of movement and excitement to learning names. If the games get unsafe in any way, drop them down a level until students demonstrate that they can manage the fun.

Level 1. In the ensemble circle, Student A makes eye contact with someone across from them and asks, "Student B, may we switch spots?" Student B MUST respond, "Yes, Student A, we may switch spots." This continues one pair at a time.

Level 2: The same movement of switching spots occurs, but this occurs nonverbally. Student A makes eye contact with Student B and nonverbally agrees to switch spots. This continues one pair at a time.

Level 3. The same movement of nonverbally changing spots. This time, add a person in the middle (Student C) who tries to steal the spot of Student A or B as they are switching spots. If Student C is successful in stealing Student A's spot, then Student A moves into the middle, and the game continues.

Wind Blows (Grades 3–8)

This game requires you to have a set number of spaces either in a circle or in chairs. Be sure to establish this before starting.

Level 1. Student A goes into the middle of the circle and states one thing true about themselves <u>that they are proud to share</u> by completing the phrase: "The wind blows for anyone who _____." All of those in the circle who have that item in common leave their spot and choose another one. The person left without a spot is now in the middle. The facilitator can decide if students can take the spot right next to them or have to cross the circle.

Level 3. Change the phrase from "The wind blows for anyone who ____" to "The wind blows for anyone who wishes for _____" or "The wind blows for anyone who also wonders _____." Get creative with your phrases!

Level 3. As students get to know one another and one another's accomplishments, they can name someone else's proud moments or wishes when they take their turn.

Witches/Wizards/Trolls (Grades 2–8)
This game is an active version of Rock, Paper, Scissors, where participants use their whole bodies instead of their hands.

Level 1. Divide the class into two groups. Quickly establish and review the poses for each group (Wizards will have a high pose; witches will have a medium height pose, and trolls will have a low height pose). Each group has 15 seconds to decide which of the three characters they would like to be. Instructor says 3, 2, 1, show me. All of Group A will hit the pose they agreed upon, and all of Group B will hit the pose they agreed upon. Wizards beat Witches, Witches beat Trolls, Trolls beat Wizards. In other words, high beats medium, medium beats low, and low beats high. Each win scores one point; play to 5 or 7.

Level 2. Add a movement and/or sounds to each pose.

Level 3. Establish safe zones for each group behind a designated line. After the group strikes the pose and wins, members of the group can try to tag them before they get back to the safe zone. Anyone who is tagged joins the winning group. The game ends when all of the players are in one group.

Points of Contact (Grades 1–5)
Level 1. Divide the class into groups of 3, 4 or 5. Quickly explain that a point of contact is a part of the body on the floor – for example, hand, foot, bottom, back, head). Be sure the group all know each other's names. Give the group a number of points of contact to accomplish. Start easy so you know they understand the concept.

Level 2. Raise the number of points of contact and/or limit the body parts that can be used. For example, say participants cannot use their hands or that they have to link to the others in the group.

Level 3. Use short answers to equations to determine the points of contact (i.e., 2+2=4).

Buddy (Grades K-8)
Level 1. Students nonverbally walk around the space without touching anyone else. The facilitator says, "Freeze," and then gives instructions on what the students should do next (make eye contact, shake hands, say hello). The facilitator says, "Freeze."

The person you are standing near is now your Elbow buddy. Introduce yourself to your Elbow buddy. Continue the activity the next time the buddy they find (a new person) will be their Pinky Buddy. Continue the activity the next time the buddy they find (a new person) will be their Toe Buddy. Ask students to find their Elbow buddy and give them a conversation topic. Repeat this with their Pinky and Toe buddy – the level of conversation gets a bit deeper and more related to the topic each time.

Cross the Room (Grades K-8)
Level 1. Students are divided in half, with each half standing against one side of the room. Students are asked a series of questions, and if it is true about them, they cross to the other side (example: "If you like pizza," "If you like going to the movies").

Level 2. Use increasingly complex, age-appropriate questions (i.e., if students have ever been victims of prejudice, felt angry, etc.).

Level 3. Use curriculum content to create questions and utilize them as a formative assessment.

Two to Your Right (Grades K-8)
Level 1. Standing in a circle, students go around and introduce themselves. The instructor stands in the middle, approaches a student, and asks them to identify the person by name two to their right. The student must complete this task before the instructor in the middle counts to ten. If the student is successful, the instructor moves on. If the student is unsuccessful, they go into the middle, and the game continues.

Level 2. The center person can change the direction and how many students are over (i.e., three to the left, six to the right).

Three Poses (Grades K-8)
Level 1. Divide the class into two groups. Quickly establish the poses for each group – something easy that everyone in the room can do, like hands on hips. Quickly review the poses and make sure everyone in the group can physically complete the poise. Each group has five seconds to decide which of the three poses they would like to do. Everyone in the small group must have

the same poise. The goal is to see how many times it takes the entire class to be doing the same pose.

Level 2. Add movement and/or sounds to the poses.

Ensemble in the Community

How to Include Families

While the school community cannot participate in daily activities connecting with one another on a personal level, there are some opportunities to share the concept and process with families. Here are some ideas:

- Students are encouraged to teach their ensemble games to their families
- Use social media to promote ensemble games
- When hosting a school event (either classroom, grade level, multi-grade, or whole school), capitalize on a transition time to invite adults to play simple ensemble games where they introduce themselves to one another and share one thing about themselves.

Continue to use your established systems of parent communication, but be sure to highlight the key moves you are making with the arts.

4

Arts Integration into Core Content Instruction

> I use tableaux all the time to strengthen literacy skills. I will do a read aloud with my students and then, in groups, have them create a tableaux identifying the beginning, middle, and end of a story, and then they share with the class who needs to also name the section of the story. **Kindergarten Teacher**

The second tenet of the Immersive Arts Integration model is the integration of the arts into the core content instruction. This requires a teacher's knowledge of core content, a deep understanding of four theatre strategies, and the ability to bridge the two. Each standards-based lesson includes the following components: standard, objective, warm-up that includes the theatre strategy, mini-lesson, activity, reflection, and assessment. The four theatre strategies are tableaux, pantomime, walking in space, and improvisation. When core content and theatre strategies are routinely paired together, lessons become engaging and result in a rigorous demonstration of comprehension.

Theatre Strategies Overview

Key New Learning for Staff
The four main theatre strategies that all staff will need to know and use are tableaux, pantomime, walking in space, and improvisation. These strategies are simple for teachers to understand, practice, and apply to the educational process. There is no need for an extensive background in theatre to learn the strategies. With thoughtful planning on engaging and enjoyable professional development, there is a short turnaround between learning the strategies and applying them to planning and pedagogy.

These strategies were intentionally selected because they are easily accessible by both teacher and student and can be used with any core content subject. They can easily be adapted to remediate or advance student learning; they are particularly effective in engaging multilingual learners and students with disabilities as they allow all students to enter the work from their comfort level and ability while also challenging them in a personalized manner.

Remember, they are *not* used as culminating activities. Rather, they are used as *the* activities. They are not used as a "final project" to showcase comprehension; they are used to deepen comprehension through the theatrical process on a daily basis.

It is worth noting to those unfamiliar with theatre that the rehearsal process (all the steps that take place before a performance) is truly where the work happens. This is where folks wrestle with all the elements that feed into character, plot development, concepts, social issues, and a myriad of other variables associated with core content.

Impact of the Model

Increasing Cognitive Load
While all aspects of the model are vital, this component is the heart of the model because it shapes students' interaction with core content throughout their day. Using tableaux, pantomime,

walking in space, and improvisation allows for active and engaging lesson tasks. This is a departure from a typical arts approach where arts integration happens only in the arts classrooms or during infrequent performances. In this model, students are immersed in the process on a daily basis.

There are several frameworks that describe gradients of cognitive load that take place during an instructional task. For the purpose of this discussion, we'll use Bloom's Taxonomy of Learning. Bloom describes the following cognitive complexities of instructional tasks in order from least to most complex:

- Remember
- Understand
- Apply
- Analyze
- Evaluate
- Create

In a traditional classroom, students may be required to refer to a text to answer a question about it. This would be a low level instructional task because it involves remembering and perhaps understanding. In many low-performing schools and/or classrooms, students typically get a watered down version of the curriculum with low level tasks. Immersive Arts Integration is a comprehensive solution to that problem. When presented with any one of the four theatre strategies, students are, at the very least, remembering, understanding, applying, and creating. This automatically increases student access to a higher cognitive load.

Emotional Connection to Learning

How Character Connections Enhance Comprehension

In addition to engaging students in cognitively demanding tasks, there is an increase in students' emotional connection to learning. Inherent in theatrical work is the need for the actor to understand the emotional state of the character they are portraying. Asking a student to create a tableaux of a historical figure or fictional character asks them to connect with that character on an emotional level immediately. All four of the strategies require the students to make a choice as to the emotional state of their character at the moment they are asked to portray. When a student creates a statue with their body that is happy because they were portraying a child being reunited with their family while studying the great migration, that child will forever be connected to that experience because they exemplified the feeling. It is imperative that students not only have an integrated approach to the overall curriculum concepts they are learning but also that they maintain an emotional connection to their learning. It is through the four theatre strategies that students begin to embody the learning. They either become the character in a story; they become the scientific concept; and/or they move through space like a mathematical equation. This is a far cry from students sitting at desks to complete worksheets.

Student Engagement

Developing Connections to Content
Engagement is another key component of the learning experience. To ensure active engagement, the student task must be carefully crafted in such a way as to ensure it captures students' attention and ensure they interact with the content. Danielson describes engagement:

> True engagement is present when students are intellectually active and emotionally invested in learning important and challenging content, not simply when they are "busy" or "on task." The critical distinction between experiences in which students are compliant and those in which they are engaged is that in the latter, students are developing their understanding through rich learning experiences, collaboration and teamwork, and thinking and reflection.
> https://danielsongroup.org/the-framework-for-teaching/

The identified theatre strategies were selected because they either require or can be adapted to accommodate collaboration. Both tableaux and improvisation must involve at least two students. Walking in space and pantomime can be done by one student but can also accommodate any number of students, depending on the assignment. There is rarely an instance where a theatre strategy would be assigned a task that would elicit only one answer. Therefore, by nature, students are collaborating with content in unplanned ways.

Now that you understand the context of and basis for the theatre strategies, let's jump into what they are and how to use them. The following chart gives you a brief overview of all strategies, followed by a more in-depth discussion of them with examples.

Tableaux

A Simple and Versatile Technique

Tableaux is defined as a dynamic frozen picture that uses levels (high, medium, low) and has a clear audience. In a theatre, you might think of Peter Pan as an example. Wendy might be on the low level sitting on the floor with John and Michael when Peter Pan comes in the window and stands on the window sill behind them on a medium level, and Tinker Bell flies in the air on a high level. The scene is created on a stage facing the audience, and the audience is seated in the theatre facing the stage. In a classroom, you might replicate the scene with a student sitting on the ground, one in a chair, and one standing. The tableaux is

TABLE 4.1 Theatre Strategies for Core Content Instruction

Tableaux	Pantomime	Walking in Space	Improvisation
A dynamic frozen picture that uses levels (high, medium, low) and has a clear audience. You can have a tableaux express a literal or abstract idea (i.e. first day of school or happiness).	Non-verbal indication of an object or action utilizing weight, height, size, length, and texture.	Non-verbal activity whereby students begin to shake off their day and themselves and move in space as a character.	Utilizing the basic rules of no denial and always adding information, students create dialogue on the spot and without a script.

created in a central classroom location, and peers are grouped in the classroom facing them. To achieve levels would require at least two or three students. However, students could also create a frozen picture individually.

Tableaux can be used to express a literal concept or abstract idea (i.e., first day of school or happiness). This versatile technique can be used in any content area; it does not necessarily require any props or materials; and is extremely efficient in terms of time. This is a great strategy to use if you're trying to gauge student comprehension of a concept in a quick, efficient, and quiet way. In terms of energy level and classroom management, it's silent, and students are not moving, so it's the quietest of the four strategies. In terms of audience experience, it requires visual attention.

Here are some more classroom examples of tableaux in a core content area:

Pantomime

Yes, that Kind of Pantomime

Pantomime is defined as a non-verbal indication of an object or action utilizing weight, height, size, length, or texture. Whereas tableaux was frozen, pantomime utilizes movement to convey the concept. In order for students to move their bodies to convey a concept, they must understand the concept and think about ways to demonstrate it using movement. This is a great strategy to use with key vocabulary words in any content area. It is more active than tableaux because it involves movement, but it is silent and the movement is contained in the object being communicated. In terms of audience experience, it requires visual attention.

Here are some classroom examples of pantomime in a core content area:

Walking in Space

More Like Walking Around the Classroom

Walking in space describes a non-verbal activity during which students adopt the persona (gestures, gait, attitude, expressions,

TABLE 4.2 Sample Tableaux Lesson Activities

Grade and Content Area	Standard	Lesson Activity
Literacy 5th Grade	RL5.2 Students are able to talk about how a character changes from beginning to end.	The class is divided into three groups. Group 1 develops a tableaux that represents the character at the beginning of the story, Group 2 creates a tableaux representing the character's arc in the middle of the story, and Group 3 creates a tableaux for the arc of the character at the end of the story. Groups present to each other.
Science 2nd Grade	2-LS4-1 Biological Evolution: Unity and Diversity Make observations of plants and animals to compare the diversity of life in different habitats.	Students are assigned to one of five groups (forest, grassland, desert, mountain, polar region, aquatic habitat). Groups create a tableaux of at least one plant and animal in the habitat.
Math Kindergarten	K.G.6 Geometry Analyze, compare, create, and compose shapes. Compose simple shapes to form larger shapes. For example, "Can you join these two triangles with full sides touching to make a rectangle?"	Students create triangles individually using their arms, then with a partner, using both sets of arms to demonstrate smaller and larger shapes.
Social Studies 7th Grade	CT.3. Geography: Human Systems: Students will interpret spatial patterns of human migration, economic activities, and political units in Connecticut, the nation, and the world. 3.3. Analyze the formation, characteristics, and functions of urban, suburban, and rural settlements.	Students are assigned to urban, suburban, and rural settlement groups. They will develop a tableaux to show the characteristics of their settlement.

TABLE 4.3 Sample Pantomime Lesson Activities

Pantomime Lesson Examples

Grade and Content Area	Standard	Lesson Activity
Literacy 7th	CCSS.ELA-LITERACY.RL.7.3 Analyze how particular elements of a story or drama interact (e.g., how the setting shapes the characters or plot).	Students will select an inanimate object that had a significant impact on the plot development and develop a pantomime to convey the object. Students will guess what object is conveyed.
Science 5th	5-LS2-1 Ecosystems: Interactions, Energy, and Dynamics Develop a model to describe the movement of matter among plants, animals, decomposers, and the environment.	Students are assigned to one of four groups (plants, animals, decomposers, and the environment). They are to devise a pantomime depicting the movement of their group. Other students will guess what they are depicting.
Math 2nd Grade	2.MD.10 Measurement and Data Represent and interpret data. Draw a picture graph and a bar graph (with single unit scale) to represent a data set with up to four categories. Solve simple put-together, take-apart, and compare problems using information presented in a bar graph.	The class can select a topic to explore (favorite lunch menu choices, favorite pets, etc.). They will create a bar graph using grid lines on the classroom floor and students as data points. Students will make observations about the data.
Social Studies 3rd	3.6. Describe the impact of various technological developments on the local community and on the nation.	Students will learn about important historical figures that helped invent technological innovations (helicopter, sewing machine, telephone, submarine, typewriter, etc.). They will then develop a pantomime to demonstrate the invention.

> I have them pantomime vocabulary words all the time, and even when I do not ask them to, I see them in groups, moving their bodies to remember a word or to explain a definition to a classmate. There are vocabulary words in all the subject areas, so we use that in all content areas. **Kindergarten Grade Teacher**

speed) of a character and move about the space as if they were the character. Imagine tasking someone who is walking 20 feet from one side of the room to another. Now imagine them doing it as a sloth, a celebrity, someone who has received sad news, a weather person, or a mad scientist. Each of those characters would embody very different approaches to the same task. Again, it requires the students to have a deep understanding of the character in order to create movement.

This strategy is useful when you want students to develop a deep connection with a character. So, you would most likely use it during a language arts or social studies lesson. The activity level is higher than tableaux or pantomime because it involves more movement, but it is still silent. You'll decide if you want everyone walking in space all at once, in small groups, or individually. In terms of audience experience, it requires visual attention.

Improvisation

Like Acting, but Without a Script

Improvisation is the most complex of the four strategies. It involves students creating dialogue on the spot and without a script. The strategy typically involves one or more people. There are a few basic ground rules, including that members of the ensemble must build upon the dialogue of their partner and cannot decline what is presented to them in any way.

This strategy presents a unique opportunity for comprehension and social emotional learning in a school setting. In order to dialogue about a concept while in their role as a character, students need to understand the concept and the character well enough to create a portrayal in the moment. In addition, it also presents a unique opportunity for students to practice collaboration and turn-taking.

This is a great strategy to use when you want students to depict a story or create then depict what they envision happened before or after the given story. This technique has the highest energy level since it involves both movement and dialogue. In terms of audience experience, it requires both visual and auditory attention.

TABLE 4.4 Sample Walking in Space Lesson Activities

Walking in Space Lesson Examples

Grade and Content Area	Standard	Lesson Activity
Literacy Kinder	CCSS.ELA-LITERACY.RL.K.2 With prompting and support, retell familiar stories, including key details.	After reading a story so that it is familiar, students will select one character from the story to embody. Students will parade in line through the classroom as their character, then land in one of two predetermined spots in the room with the other students who embody that character.
Science 7th	MS-PS2-1 Motion and Stability: Forces and Interactions Apply Newton's Third Law to design a solution to a problem involving the motion of two colliding objects.	Students will work in small groups to design protective safety padding for skateboarding or any other given sport. They will discuss what physical reactions might happen if two students collide with one another at a series of given body parts (elbow to elbow, knee to knee, hip to foot, etc.) or with a stationary object (head to wall or wrist to ground) then pantomime the actions without the protective padding then with the protective padding.
Math 5th	5.G.2 Geometry Graph points on the coordinate plane to solve real-world and mathematical problems. 5.G.A.2 Represent real-world and mathematical problems by graphing points in the first quadrant of the coordinate plane and interpret coordinate values of points in the context of the situation.	Students will create a coordinate plane using painter's tape on the floor. This is best done in a large space such as a cafeteria or hallway. Students can then complete a variety of activities on the grid, including completing given equations or creating equations for peers.
Social Studies 2nd	4.5. Explain ways in which humans use and interact with environments.	Students will discuss that humans depend on, adapt, and modify the environment. Examples of use include deforestation, energy resources, water use, waste, pollution, and urban expansion. Students are assigned to one of six groups. Half the group will pantomime as the environment, and the other half will pantomime as the human impacting the environment.

TABLE 4.5 Sample Improvisation Lesson Activities

Improvisation Lesson Examples

Grade and Content Area	Standard	Lesson Example
Literacy 2nd	CCSS.ELA-LITERACY.RL.2.2 Recount stories, including fables and folktales from diverse cultures, and determine their central message, lesson, or moral.	Students will read a variety of stories in a genre. They will then select their favorite book and tell.
Science Kinder	K-ESS3-2 Earth and Human Activity Ask questions to obtain information about the purpose of weather forecasting to prepare for and respond to severe weather.	Students will learn about various types of weather in their area (i.e., sunny, rainy, windy, etc.). Weather types are written on cards and placed in a basket. Students will select a card, then improvise their weather forecast in character as a local television weather reporter.
Math 7th	7.RP.1 Analyze proportional relationships and use them to solve real-world and mathematical problems. Compute the rates associated with ratios of fractions, including ratios of lengths, areas, and other quantities measured in like or different units. For example, if a person walks ½ mile in each ¼ hour, compute the unit rate as the complex fraction 1/2/1/4 miles per hour, equivalently 2 miles per hour.	Students will work as a whole class and in small groups to determine how each small group might stagger their start times and paces so as to arrive at a finish line at the end of the hallway at the same time, then write those rates as ratios of fractions.
Social Studies 5th	3.2. Explain how roles and status of people have differed and changed throughout history based on gender, age, class, racial and ethnic identity, wealth, and/or social position.	Students will research a variety of historical figures. They will select one person and develop a character sketch based on their demographic information. Students will interview one another in character to demonstrate the differences between their experiences. This can be done in presentation format in front of peers, a larger audience, or in pairs concurrently.

> One of the things that I . . . brag about is the comprehension piece and how, in kindergarten, we use theatre and retelling to cement comprehension. I have kids that I've done things at the very beginning of the year, last year. You know, the year before, "Who can retell a story today, just like they did two years ago?" So that's what I brag about. And I lend out my materials to new teachers, my masks or my costumes or a set piece or, you know, simple things, really simple little things that get the kids engaged. And so they create all their own things. Which also, of course, helps retell. Yeah, that's amazing. **Immersive Arts Integration Teacher**

Putting It All Together

Four Strategies in One Lesson

To illustrate examples of the strategies, here is a sample lesson plan written for middle school students around their study of immigration and World War II using the book The Arrival by Shaun Tan. Here is a description of the book by its author:

> *The Arrival* is a migrant story told as a series of wordless images. A man leaves his wife and child in an impoverished town, seeking better prospects in an unknown country on the other side of a vast ocean. . . . With nothing more than a suitcase and a handful of currency, the immigrant must find a place to live, food to eat and some kind of gainful employment. He is helped along the way by sympathetic strangers, each carrying their own unspoken history: stories of struggle and survival.

The plan is presented in a narrative format instead of the lesson plan template so that you can understand the thinking behind some of the instructional choices.

Standards

Here are two examples of Social Studies standards. However, both reading and writing standards would be equally as relevant:

> HIST 8.3 Analyze multiple factors that influenced the perspectives of people during different historical eras.

ECO 8.1 Explain how economic decisions affect the well-being of individuals, businesses, and society.

Objective

Students will be able to take the perspective of an immigrant arriving in the United States and write a letter to the immigrant's family articulating the process.

Materials

Multiple copies of the book <u>The Arrival</u> by Shaun Tan are disassembled into individual pages.

Tasks

To begin the work, students are first given a series of selected images and are asked to work collaboratively in groups of three to four to put them in order. The pictures are somewhat ambiguous and create the need for deep discussion. They are then asked to provide a title for the story and to create a tableaux of the beginning, middle, and end. This requires synthesis of the pictures. These retellings of their original stories through **tableaux** are shared with the class.

After hearing the various stories, the class collectively chooses one character to think about further. Typically, the students select the male character because it appears most frequently. Students are asked to create an identity for the character, including his name, age, family background, the world that surrounds him, and the choice that lies in front of him. Each student's detail builds upon the next until they have created a context around the character. The teacher can write down these characteristics on the board for visual support. They are also asked to think about how the external world would make this character feel on the inside, and they share those adjectives with the class. These activities allow space for students to imagine details about the character to make him more real to them. Students are then asked to briefly embody the character in a frozen image once again using the new details. Then, they start to move that image about the space. As they are **walking in space**, they are taken through guided imagery of what the man must feel like walking home from his last day of work, knowing that that evening, he is beginning his journey to a new land. Students often walk tentatively and tensely around the space.

The teacher then continues the guided facilitation of the students in the space and in the role. They use **pantomime** to pack their suitcase with three belongings to take on the train with them. This requires them to think about which items they might take in their situation and why. They are asked to feel the weight of the objects and endow them with emotions. Once their suitcase is full, they close it and carry it back to the kitchen.

Next, students are asked to find one partner, and through **improvisation**, they are asked to have a conversation in the role between the man and a family member about his decision to immigrate to a new land. Through this exercise, students must make many informed decisions in the moment. Who is their character? What is their relationship? How do they feel about the news of him leaving? After a minute to prepare, the students engage in an improvisational scene. Students participated in this activity several times.

Students then reflect. They are asked what else they learned about their character in this process and to reconnect to the first male character and adjust their physicality with the release or addition of burden based on those conversations. The lesson concludes with one volunteer student remaining in the role of the male character walking through the train station and the rest of the class engaging in all the strategies to create a train station soundscape. Once the main character moves through the train station, the class once again reflects on how he must feel, and one last time, everyone reconnects with the character and discusses his emotional being.

Students then find a quiet spot and continue in character. They write a short letter home to the family to let them know of the arrival. This writing prompt allows students yet another opportunity to make meaning of the experience and to engage their critical and creative thinking as they recall the journey they have just endured. As you can imagine, the students' writing is robust and filled with sensory details that likely would not have existed without the character exploration using the four theatre strategies.

Assessment: The teacher has the option of grading the student's letter in character or providing students with a separate assessment task. In either case, the objectives and rubric should be shared at the start of the unit and the book will need to be placed in its appropriate historical context. Students will need to analyze the factors that influenced the perspective of the main character in this book and explain how economic decisions affected his well-being. The teacher may also choose to grade the student's skill as related to the theatre strategies.

As you can see, this lesson is significantly more complex and comprehensive than students simply reading a book and talking about it with their teacher or peers. The process of taking the perspective of the character and then embodying the character creates a profound and deep connection to the character's experience. When the writing task is introduced, students have a wealth of detail from which to draw.

Now that you have a sense of the strategies and how they might be used, let's take a look at how teachers learn to use them.

> Teachers see the results. When they see not just test scores, but they see student engagement . . . student interest, and students that are happy to walk in the classroom . . . we're all amazing teachers here but . . . when [students] know there's going to be the opportunity for them to present and create and explore it has an effect on their overall attitude and perception towards school and learning.
> **3rd Grade Teacher**

Professional Development

Teaching Theatre Novices

Early on in the development of this model, it became apparent that, for the teachers to feel confident in planning integrated lessons, they needed a strong understanding of the strategies and that the strategies needed to be presented in clear and digestible ways. For a seasoned arts educator (particularly theatre arts), the use of tableaux, pantomime, walking in space, and improvisation are not monumental. However, for a teacher new to this process, the four strategies are simple to learn and then easily integrated into their existing instructional practices with well-crafted professional development. They also serve as the four main groups of eventual more complex theatre integration work. We'll present the ideal professional development model in terms of staffing and timing, but it can be adapted based on your circumstances. You'll start with a one to two hour introductory session to present an overview of the four strategies. Staff of all roles should participate so they gain a broad understanding of expectations. Generally speaking, each strategy is explained, staff practices it using familiar stories (i.e., the Three Little Pigs, etc.), and then staff presents it to one another. If there is any initial hesitation by staff, it will quickly dissolve into laughter as they collaborate on their vignettes.

After the introductory session, there will be four sessions (ideally one hour in length) for each of the strategies. During these sessions, classroom teachers, specialists, and special education resource teachers learn the strategies in more depth. Just like the introductory session, staff will review the strategy, practice it using familiar stories, and then present it to colleagues as a quick reminder. They will then break into grade level groups and develop a lesson using their current curriculum. It will be very important to give them time for this so they can start to see how it's connected to what they do daily. Eventually, the classroom teachers will be expected to design lessons and use the strategies on a daily basis. The specialists will be expected to co-plan units and lessons with the classroom teachers. And the special education resource teachers may need to support students if they push into classrooms and/or if students need assistance completing assignments. They should develop a shared online document where they capture lesson plan ideas. Everyone can contribute to it.

After the broad introduction to everyone, then the in depth review with just teachers, grade levels will then participate in a month-long cycle of learning that more closely connects teachers with planning lessons using their core content. These learning cycles are facilitated by the coach and are made up of co-planning, modeling, and reflection sessions for each strategy. It is suggested that the strategies are presented to staff in order from least to most complex: tableaux, pantomime, walking in space, and improvisation. Here are the steps:

- Week 1, Session 1: Coach and all teachers on a grade level meet to identify a lesson that would lend itself to using tableaux. They co-plan the lesson.
- Week 1, Session 2: Coach teaches the lesson while all teachers observe and take notes. They all debrief about it immediately after. They may want to discuss questions such as: What went well? Why were certain choices made during the lesson? How did students respond?
- Week 2, Session 1: Coach and all teachers on the same grade level meet. Coach and Teacher A will co-plan the next lesson using tableaux with input from Teachers B and C.
- Week 2, Session 2: Teacher A teaches the lesson in Class A while the coach and Teachers B and C observe and take notes. They all debrief about it immediately after.
- Week 3, Session 1: Coach and all teachers on the same grade level meet. Coach and Teacher B will co-plan the next lesson using tableaux with input from Teachers A and C.
- Week 3, Session 2: Teacher B teaches the lesson in Class B while the coach and Teachers A and C observe and take notes. They all debrief about it immediately after.
- Week 4, Session 1: Coach and all teachers on the same grade level meet. Coach and Teacher C will co-plan the next lesson using tableaux with input from Teachers A and B.
- Week 4, Session 2: Teacher C teaches the lesson in Class C while the coach and Teachers A and B observe and take notes. They all debrief about it immediately after.

Using this model, teachers are exposed to four opportunities to co-plan and observe lessons and one opportunity to teach a lesson in front of colleagues, all with the guidance of a coach who can course correct immediately. This intense support is an effective and efficient way to learn a strategy and get immediate feedback on it in a short period of time. Because the grade levels are working together, it creates a sense of camaraderie and trust while learning the new strategies. It is not recommended that leadership attend these coaching sessions. These sessions are meant for teachers to take risks, make mistakes, and learn from them. They are not meant to be evaluative or to be used as an administrative observation opportunity. But you know your school; if it feels safe to include the leadership, then do so!

Ideally, this coaching cycle should be repeated across all grade levels and for each of the four strategies. There are some variations that should be considered. The specialists and other staff may or may not be included in these sessions depending on the relationship and whether additional staff will hinder any risk taking. The cycle takes four weeks presented with one coach and three teachers; this timeline will be extended or reduced if there are more or fewer teachers. As presented, each teacher teaches their own classroom. If the coaching rounds repeat after the initial four cycles, teachers can teach in other classrooms. And finally, teachers may consider teaching at other grade levels. This is a nice opportunity to align content vertically while practicing the strategy. At the very least, after four months, the entire teaching staff has been extensively trained and should be able to generalize their experience so they can plan lessons independently in any core content area.

Early success and immediate implementation are key to the overall success of this work. Sometimes, other initiatives spend too much time in the planning phases. Educators have a tendency

TABLE 4.6 Professional Development Timeline

Session Number	Professional Development Session	Suggested Time
PD 1	Foundations of the Work/Setting Up Space	Summer Prior to starting the work
PD 2	Shared Artistic Experience	August
PD 3	Shared Arts Education Experience	September
PD 4	Ensemble Building	September
PD 5	Tableaux	October
PD 6	Pantomime	November
PD 7	Walking in Space	December
PD 8	Improvisation	January
PD 9	Building Integrated Lesson Plans	February
PD 10	Creating Integrated Units of Study	March

to focus on all the possible roadblocks when experimenting with a new model. This can delay their gratification with the power of the experience. In the Immersive Arts Integration model, the teachers are required to try the strategies right away in their teaching. Because they are heavily supported and there is no judgment if mistakes are made, they will quickly experience success and be motivated to continue the work.

Lesson Planning

How Is It Different in This Model?

Once teachers know the strategies, it's time to include them in the lesson plans. Most certified teachers will be well-versed in lesson planning, and there are many templates and models that articulate the process. The steps include identifying the standards and objectives, designing the task, selecting the materials, and assessing. The task design could include modeling, guided practice, and independent practice. These task design options can be ordered differently depending on how the teacher wants the student to access the content. In a more constructivist approach, the teacher may opt to start with independent practice, support with guided practice, and then close the lesson with modeling to solidify the learning. In the Immersive Arts Integration model, the task design phase is unique because the teacher will select one of four main theatre strategies that most closely align with the intended lesson outcome and incorporate it into the lesson. There is an additional discussion of lesson planning in Chapter 5.

Planning for Diverse Learners

Pair Students with Curated Strategies

Knowing and valuing students' unique contributions to the learning space is a key component of good teaching. Many students are multilingual learners or have disabilities. The use of theatre strategies can be an inclusive practice when implemented appropriately. Students with diverse needs often benefit from

TABLE 4.7 Theatre Strategy Implementation Expectation and Cycles of Support

Session Number	Strategy	Suggested Month	Implementation Expectations and Cycles of Support
PD 5	Tableaux	October	♦ Learn strategy in Professional Development ♦ Modeled in their classroom by arts integration specialist ♦ Observe peers trying out the strategy ♦ Facilitate the strategy under observation of arts integration specialist ♦ Use once at least once a week in classroom teaching
PD 6	Pantomime	November	♦ Reflect on the use of tableaux ♦ Learn pantomime strategy in Professional Development ♦ Modeled in their classroom by arts integration specialist ♦ Observe peers trying out the strategy ♦ Facilitate the strategy under observation of arts integration specialist ♦ Use once at least once a week in classroom teaching
PD 7	Walking in Space	December	♦ Reflect on use of pantomime ♦ Learn walking in space strategy in Professional Development ♦ Modeled in their classroom by arts integration specialist ♦ Observe peers trying out the strategy ♦ Facilitate the strategy under observation of arts integration specialist ♦ Use once at least once a week in classroom teaching
PD 8	Improvisation	January	♦ Reflect on the use of walking in space ♦ Learn improvisation in Professional Development ♦ Modeled in their classroom by arts integration specialist ♦ Observe peers trying out the strategy ♦ Facilitate the strategy under observation of arts integration specialist ♦ Use once at least once a week in classroom teaching
		February	♦ Reflect on use of improvisation

small group work, project based learning, active learning, rehearsal opportunities, and the opportunity to represent their understanding orally and with movement. A teacher's thorough knowledge of their students will allow for the content to be paired with a strategy that works for the particular group of students in a class. Here are some scaffolds to consider:

- Physical set up of the room
- Visual supports
- Translation of key vocabulary
- Working with a partner
- Opportunity to rehearse

The age of the students must be considered as well. Kindergarteners may have a difficult time maintaining appropriate personal space. Middle school students may be squeamish about being assigned to create a tableaux with certain peers. Fourth graders may turn every interaction into an opportunity to make a joke at a peer's expense. The teacher will need to establish clear boundaries and explicitly teach them to ensure the developmental idiosyncrasies of the age group have been considered.

Assessment

Core Content and Arts Strategies

Consideration should be made regarding assessing both the core content and the arts strategies. At some point in the process, students should demonstrate an understanding of the theatre strategies. The amount of time spent learning or reviewing the four strategies at the lesson launch should decrease within the year and over the years. In the beginning, students should be able to name and define the strategies. As time goes on, students should be able to name which strategy best exemplifies the learning they mastered.

Assessment continues to happen with both formative and summative assessments measuring the progress toward mastery of standards. The summative assessment process will be discussed further in Chapter 5. In terms of daily and weekly assessments, teachers will continue to check for understanding throughout the lesson when students are engaged in the theatre activities. Students may use the four strategies to demonstrate content comprehension and mastery, and it should be evident that they capture it accurately. For example, groups of five students may use pantomime to dramatize the concept of force and motion on a playground. One group can be on the swings, another on the slide, another on a seesaw, etc. The group must also write a summary paragraph describing their assigned concept and how they chose to demonstrate it. The audience is charged with naming the force and using appropriate academic language. During the process, the teacher should rotate through the classroom, checking for understanding, providing feedback, and taking data on student comprehension to inform future instructional decisions. After the pantomime, students take a traditional test to demonstrate their comprehension of the concepts. There are several options and ways to assess them in this example. The teacher must decide whether to assess content only or add components of performance. This will depend on the length of time students have been using the theatre strategies, the state and local standards for presentation, and/or the community expectations regarding what students should know and be able to do. The teacher can assess only the content knowledge through the traditional test, only the ability of the group to convey their concept; the group's ability to work together; participation; the accuracy of the written description; and/or all of these. Ideally, students will need to participate in developing the assessment by creating the rubric.

Teacher Supervision Versus Teacher Evaluation

Accountability Is Not a Scary Word
Now that teachers have been taught the four theatre strategies, have participated in the initial round of coaching cycles, and are writing lesson plans to capture their work, what are the implications for ensuring the work is implemented with fidelity and positively impacts students? How do leaders support teachers in taking risks while simultaneously evaluating their

practice? Leaders must strike a balance to ensure teachers have all the tools and practice they need before evaluating them on the integrated strategies. Here is a list of look-fors to consider when ensuring professional learning is being put into place:

- Lesson plans indicating which theatre strategies are used in the lesson
- Anchor charts of the four theatre strategies posted in the classroom
- Students use key vocabulary throughout the day (ensemble, actor neutral, tableaux, walking in space, pantomime, improvisation)
- Posted objectives that include both core content standards and integrated arts standards

There's always the question of how much and how often. The answer depends on the preexisting skill set and the amount of professional development. Generally speaking, leaders should reward teachers for trying the strategies, whether they are successful or not). In the beginning and for teachers new to the practice, the expectation would be one to two attempted theatre integration strategies per week. At full implementation, the expectations would be one to two theatre integration strategies per day. Teacher evaluation models do not explicitly name the strategies used, rather, they focus on the impact on students. Therefore, it is acceptable to acknowledge the effort to try the theatre strategies.

At some point in the learning process, teachers will be responsible for teaching the strategies correctly and using them in meaningful ways. The leader will need to identify the tipping point (when in the process), and teachers become responsible for full and effective implementation. Again, this decision will be based on the context of the building. The recommendation is to *first reward the effort and then reward the execution*. During this implementation phase, it is important to remember that there is a whole scale system shift. So, students will be learning while teachers are learning while the coach is supporting both. These simultaneous efforts will ensure the model's sustainability.

The administrator and/or leadership team will need to transparently determine how and when the theatre strategies will become part of the expected instructional practice. It may help the team to think about best teaching practices in general. One of the hallmarks of exemplary instruction is the ability of a teacher to ask questions in such a way that elicits multiple answers, encourages students to develop hypotheses, makes connections, and challenges them to think about the concept in new ways. Challenging students to walk in space as a character or to create a tableaux to demonstrate a concept puts them in a position of having to internalize the content to externalize the learning. Participating in an activity such as a living museum (a combination of walking in space, pantomime, and improvisation) requires the student to engage peers through questioning and dialogue. In this way, it is not only the teacher asking the questions but the students as well.

In its most evolved form, instructional feedback should be provided from teacher to teacher. As we discussed earlier in the chapter, peer feedback is built into the professional development design. As teachers move through the cycles of learning, they are teaching in front of their grade level peers and providing feedback to one another. Once the cycles of learning are complete, a decision can be made to continue the cycles as part of the routine professional development process. Ideally, these cycles become part of how the school does business.

Now that teachers know how to use tableaux, pantomime, walking in space, and improvisation with core content lessons, we'll explore how to create integrated units of study in Chapter 5.

Immersive Arts Integration Lesson Components

> **Warm-Up**: The first activity of the class that allows you to access the children and get them up on their feet. It also allows you to manage the energy in the room (perhaps after lunch, you need to center them, or if it is during the first period, you may need to wake them up (approximately 5 minutes).

> **Prep-Activity** (also referred to as the mini lesson): Provides students with the concepts/vocabulary they need to achieve the goals of the main lesson successfully (approximately 10 minutes).
>
> **Main Activity:** This is where the ARTS INTEGRATION HAPPENS. This is where students are able to practice/experience the content that was introduced in the Mini Lesson. Students are actively engaged in MAKING MEANING of the concepts (approximately 15–25 minutes).
>
> **Share Out of Learning:** This is a unique feature of the Arts Integration model, as it is important for students to share their learning and the work they did in the main activity (approximately 10 minutes).
>
> **Reflection**: Students must discuss what they did and what effect it had on them. This can be as a share out, journaling, share with a neighbor, or draw a picture. Remember, the final reflection of the day relates back to the guiding question or aim and links how this class impacts the Unit goals (approximately 5 minutes).

Third Grade Lesson Sample

Now that you've seen the template, let's put it into action with a sample lesson. These third graders are in a unit studying figurative language and moving toward using it in their own writing. Figurative language is defined as simile, metaphor, personification, and hyperbole.

> **Standards:**
>
> National Core Arts Standards: TH 1:2, 4:1
> Common Core State Standards in ELA: CCSS SL: 3; CCSS W: 4

Learning Objective:

- Define simile, metaphor, personifications, and hyperbole
- Identify simile, metaphor, personifications, and hyperbole
- Write their own examples of simile, metaphor, personifications, and hyperbole

Warm-Up: Flamingo, Bologna Sandwich, Disco Party Ensemble Game

Direct Instruction: Teacher reviews the definitions of simile, metaphor, hyperbole, and personification

Simile:

- At dinner, I am as hungry AS a wolf.
- This summer we went to the beach, and it was as hot AS an oven.
- Ella Fitzgerald sang like a bird.

Metaphor:

- Henri Matisse was a master painter; the paintbrush was a magic wand in his hand.
- The curtain of night fell, and we knew it was bedtime.
- The day before summer break, the classroom was a zoo.

Hyperbole:

- I'm so hungry I could eat a horse.
- I walked a million miles to get here.
- The person was as tall as my house.

Personification:

- Lightning danced across the sky.
- The wind screamed in the night.
- The last piece of pie was calling my name.
- My alarm clock yells at me to get out of bed every morning.

Main Activity: Students use the same concepts from the Warm-Up but instead use the four concepts of the lesson (when hyperbole, students make exaggerated motions).

- Break the class into groups of four or five.
- Give each group an envelope. In the envelope are strips of paper with one example of each form of figurative language.
- Students need to first properly identify them. Second, they need to create a tableaux of each phrase. Third, when ready, the teacher will say "simile," and each group will show their tableaux of a simile to demonstrate understanding.
- Finally, the groups will be asked to create examples of their own simile, metaphor, personification, and hyperbole AND then create either a tableaux for each OR a short scene with improvised lines to show each.

Share Out: Each group will share their original phrases in either tableaux or pantomime.

Reflection: How does the use of figurative language enhance our own writing? OR As a reader, how might the use of figurative language enhance the story?

5

Creating Integrated Units of Study

> The cycles of implementation and peer feedback didn't feel threatening in that space, which is so different from other observations and really because the onus is on the kids. It's really about you being able to see what the kids are understanding. Really, you can see it because if I didn't teach it right, they wouldn't be able to do it . . . . Is that different from other initiatives and models? Yes, yeah. 100%.
> **Kindergarten Teacher**

The third tenet of the Immersive Arts Integration model is the creation of integrated units of study. This collaborative process joins core content teachers and arts specialists. Teachers identify key curriculum ideas of the content areas, while arts specialists identify authentic opportunities to infuse arts as an instructional vehicle. Teacher teams follow a 7 step protocol to find areas of overlap and map out the teaching and learning process. This approach results in more efficient teaching and allows students to make deeper connections as they see cross curricular connections. Culminating activities and celebrations of the work are incorporated.

What Is It?

An Antidote to a Curriculum Map or Manual
A unit of study is a group of lessons across a number of content areas. The lessons are selected so that some content areas may be highlighted or serve as a focus while others take a less central role. A unit of study does not come pre-packaged in a resource or manual because it is a unique creation based on the state and/or district curriculum, areas of interest of the teachers and/or students, available resources, or any other contributing factor relevant to the creators at this moment in time. Units can be created and adopted year after year, adjusted and improved from year to year, or abandoned when they no longer make sense. Examples of units of study might be the Mayan Civilizations, parts of speech, or changing seasons. The process of developing cross curricular units of study allows teachers to collaborate in new ways and for students to see how their learning is connected. In the Immersive Arts Integration model, the integration of academics with arts (as opposed to the addition of arts to academics) paves the way for increased engagement and comprehension. Just like the list of ensemble activities, the units of study and lesson plans are kept in a shared document. Having this living document ensures consistency across grade levels and over time. If new staff are onboarded, they will have access to the document for a smooth transition.

Who Does It?

Infusing Collaborative Teacher Planning
This collaborative process includes the classroom teacher, arts specialists (music, visual arts, theatre, etc.), leadership, and arts integration specialists. As we've previously discussed, your school or district may or may not have an arts integration specialist or coach, or you may have one that is part time or consults. If you do not have someone in this role, you can identify a grade level leader or an administrator to serve in this capacity. The person who leads the planning meetings will know the protocols, ask clarifying questions, ensure the arts specialists are contributing, and help the team troubleshoot. These planning meetings

should take place at least one month in advance of the unit so that materials, locations, and personnel can be identified and assigned. In your launch year, your first unit planning session takes place after the four theatre strategies (tableaux, pantomime, walking in space, and improvisation) have been introduced and are being used by teachers. This way, teachers will be able to spot opportunities to include them from the outset. When teachers are empowered to collaborate and create lessons, the planning process becomes organic and exciting. This is a departure from reading a teacher's manual or curriculum map and implementing it without input from colleagues or specialists.

Unit Length and Planning Frequency

A Fixed Process Yielding Flexible Units
Generally speaking, these units are between six and eight weeks long. Their length will depend on the curriculum, the standards, the length of the district's marking periods (quarters, semesters, or trimesters), and other natural breaks in the schedule due to vacations or other significant events. The unit periods do not need to be the same across all grade levels. For example, a first grade unit might take seven weeks, and a fourth grade unit might take eight weeks. This gives each grade level space to launch and celebrate the units without overlapping. The units can also vary in length. Some units may take eight weeks, and others may take five or six. It all depends on what the unit authors and school community values and wants to highlight. Planning should take place at least two months in advance of the unit to ensure materials are secured, guest speakers are identified, and celebrations are scheduled. Over the course of a nine month school year, this means there would be approximately six units.

Components of an Integrated Unit of Study

A Step by Step Method to Integrate
Step 1: Identify Content Areas and Standards
The first step is to identify how many content areas you want to integrate. Most schools have four main content areas: language

arts (reading, writing, speaking, and listening), math, social studies, and science. There are also five main arts areas: visual arts, dance, theatre, media, and music. Ideally, these would all be integrated. If you are just starting implementation, you may consider starting with a subset of content areas and then adding once you have mastered the process. In terms of the complexity of the academic core content, typically, language arts is easiest to integrate, followed by social studies, science, and then math. The arts areas are not necessarily more or less complex but will relate to the academic areas in different ways. Once you know which subjects you'll integrate, create a spreadsheet of each content area and the priority standards covered during that unit. If you are drawing from a district curriculum map, these will be easy to identify. If you are drawing from the Common Core State Standards, be sure all standards will be covered over the course of the year.

The following is a sample table that highlights Step 1 and Step 2 of the unit planning process based on a fictional third grade classroom in Groton, Connecticut. Groton is known as the "submarine capital of the world." The priority standards that relate to the topic of submarines are listed. For this example, connections were identified across three academic content and two arts areas.

Step 2: Identify Connections Between Standards

As you review your list of standards for each of the content areas, identify ways in which they may be connected. The team now has the option to think creatively about how a central theme or topic might be highlighted and serve as a launching pad to include other standards and topics. Combinations could include ancient civilizations, patterns, and haiku. Highlight these topics on your spreadsheet, and then lift them off the page onto a connected list. Alternatively, the team can identify a topic, and then select standards that can be incorporated into that topic's exploration. The key tip to remember here is that all grade level standards must be covered over the course of the year. Naturally, there will be some standards that associate with a topic or unit of study; these must be covered in isolation so that students access all of their grade level standards.

TABLE 5.1 Sample Unit Plan

Subject Area	Language Arts	Social Studies	Science	Visual Art	Theatre
STANDARD	CCSS.ELA-LITERACY.RI.3.3 Describe the relationship between a series of historical events, scientific ideas or concepts, or steps in technical procedures in a text, using language that pertains to time, sequence, and cause/effect. CCSS.ELA-Literacy.W.3.1 Write opinion pieces on topics or texts, supporting a point of view with reasons.	Students will engage in a yearlong study of Connecticut and local towns. They will analyze the impact of geography, economics, and government structures to study the history and contemporary society of Connecticut and local towns.	3-5-ETS1-1 Define a simple design problem that can be solved through the development of an object, tool, process, or system and includes several criteria for success and constraints on materials, time, or cost.	VA:Re.7.2.3a Determine messages communicated by an image. Visit local museums and view murals from local artists.	TH:Cr1.1.3. Create roles, imagined worlds, and improvised stories in a drama/theatre work.
TASK	Read non-fiction texts about submarines. Write an opinion piece.	Read primary resources and demonstrate comprehension by answering questions.	Design a submersible object using a given set of materials.	Analyze local artistic works.	Write and perform a devised script to prepare for sharing opinion pieces with legislators.

Step 3: Identify an Essential Question

Now that you've identified the standards across at least one academic content area and at least one arts form, it's time to identify an essential question. This is a very unique opportunity to think about the big picture, articulate it, and present it to students. This should be an overarching question that will guide the unit of study and will be answered by the exploration of all content areas. There is no one answer to this question. The answer will take into consideration the academic and arts content of the previous six weeks; it will be broad enough so that students may incorporate their diverse (linguistic, cultural, ethnic, racial, and other) perspectives; and it will require students to analyze and synthesize their learning. Sample questions include the following:

- How does friendship change over time?
- What is a pattern, and how do patterns help or hinder open thought?
- What does it mean to be balanced?
- How are decision makers selected?

Once you identify your question, brainstorm a list of answers to it. This will inform your unit assessment (see further on).

For our example in Groton, the submarine capital of the world, an essential question might be, "Do submarines help or harm the world?"

Step 4: Identify a Unit Launch and Celebration

Each unit of study will have an engaging and interactive launch that simultaneously prepares and excites the students (and teachers!) for the learning. Think way beyond the standard verbal introduction during which the teacher explains the unit. Consider inviting guest speakers, taking a field trip, participating in a live performance, or reading a primary resource. The launch should spark interest and curiosity. There should be a "wow" factor for both students and teachers.

The celebration is a culminating activity that encapsulates the learning and is connected to the kickoff. It presents an opportunity for students to demonstrate their academic content mastery. This should match the kickoff. In the context of an Immersive Arts Integration approach, there is an acknowledgment of the interdependence of the arts and academics and an elevation of the arts as an integral part of the learning process. These celebrations are separate from skill-based arts events such as winter concerts, school plays, or art shows. Skill-based events continue to be an important part of the school culture and will continue to take place.

In our submarine example, students might present a devised script of a pitch to lawmakers to continue to support the submarine base in Groton (this is a fictitious task). Students would include how the base would benefit the economy and help support marine exploration. An alternate presentation to lawmakers might focus on denying the submarine base application because submarines could be used as weapons. In either scenario, a rubric would be developed indicating the expected outcomes of the project which would include both academic and arts based skills in conjunction with content mastery.

Step 5: Identify the Timeline

The launch, lessons, and celebrations are plotted on a calendar. Grade levels should follow the same calendar, but the entire school does not need to do so. Definitely build in one or two extra days to allow for adjustment based on student or adult needs or interests. Here are some additional considerations for you:

- District marking period calendar
- Vacations and holidays
- Schedules of other grade levels
- Completion of content prior to summative testing
- Aligning community performances or presentations with the community calendar

The calendar may shift depending on the number of academic and arts areas being integrated.

In addition to planning the calendar across weeks and months, the daily calendar should also be planned. A traditional approach may require time devoted to each subject area daily in order to meet state and/or district requirements. Since some subjects will be combined, they will be named as such on the calendar and within the lesson plan. For example, if the lesson integrates math (integers) and walking in space (theatre), it should be listed as Math/Theatre on the unit and daily plan. This should be clear to administrators and central office staff who will evaluate.

Step 6: Plan Daily Lessons

There are many lesson plan templates and iterations. Lesson planning was discussed in Chapter 4 but will be briefly reviewed here in the context of unit planning. Once again, this discussion will highlight the major components, but they can and should be adjusted based on district requirements. The key difference in an Immersive Arts Integration lesson is the inclusion of a theatre strategy as a pedagogical tool. The strategy is not expected to be used in each and every lesson but rather in key lessons in which it elevates the learning and organically connects with the content. Lessons include warm-up (theatre strategy), direct instruction, task (during which the integration takes place), and reflection (tied to essential question):

1. Warm-up   3-4 minutes
2. Direct Instruction   5-7 minutes
3. Task/Integration   25+ minutes
4. Reflection question 2-3 minutes

Step 7: Develop Assessments

Assessment is a broad term that can refer to checking for understanding within a lesson, at the end of a lesson, at a midpoint in a unit, or at the end of a unit. Formative assessments happen within days and units and help the teacher adjust their instruction to include reteaching or recalibration of objectives based on student performance; these were discussed in Chapter 4. Summative assessments happen at the end of the unit and measure student mastery as well as inform unit plan revisions for the following year. There are three considerations for developing assessment criteria and processes. First, it is critical to ensure that students are held to the same academic and arts standards as their peers instructed with other models. The standards taught and learned are the same as with other models; only the methodology differs. Second, the academic and arts standards will be assessed. If the tasks were well-designed, there would be no concern regarding student performance. At the end of the day, all students will need to take the same high stakes tests, and this model will prepare them to do so. Third, students will have the opportunity to respond to the essential question. Since the essential questions are designed with an emphasis on analysis and synthesis, they will naturally be of higher cognitive demand. Since students are able to incorporate an art form into their learning and response, they will organically include an engaging and interactive component.

Grading systems exist at the classroom and school or district level. Unless you are teaching in a private or highly specialized school with its own grading system, teachers will likely need to grade the units of study as a classroom-based opportunity. Since the unit of study and related lesson plans are all standards-based, teachers will be able to provide grades on a school-based or district-based grading system that is also based on standards. One will feed the other. Similarly, any arts-specific element can be graded for the skill-based portion of the progress report or report card.

There may be a situation in which the progress report or report card does not capture the arts form. If you are building out your program with dance and theatre but are using a district-based report card that does not have those subject areas, the school needs to consider how progress in those areas is scored. Consideration should be made to add a skill-based progress report so that expectations and progress are clear to the student, teacher, and family. The progress reports should list an effort grade and then a rubric based on the National Core Arts Standards.

In this sample rubric, the essential questions and tasks are listed, followed by the key curriculum standards in each of the academic and arts areas. Descriptors match performance on a three point scale. The rubric is presented to students in conjunction with the unit launch so that expectations are clear. Rubrics should be given simultaneously to teachers and students so they can self-assess.

Diversity and Equity

Identity Reflections
A key benefit to the co-creation of integrated units of study is the reflection of the school community at all levels. The authors are able to hand select topics, standards, and themes that reflect what their community values, not what they are told to value by a program. In our submarine example, the spirit of the community was reflected throughout the unit. In other cities and schools, the team will choose to explore that which is meaningful to them. To take this concept further, partnerships can be formed within the community as well. Since all members of the community have unique stories based on their lived experiences, it is imperative to create opportunities for those stories to become part of the learning process in meaningful ways. This ensures the inclusion of diverse perspectives.

Planning Then Revising

Build the Plane as You Fly It
In your first year of implementation, you will spend the majority of your time learning about theatre strategies and ensemble games. Once those are established, your focus will turn to lesson planning and then unit planning. You will build the plane as you fly it; in other words, you will learn how to plan a unit by planning a unit. In this scenario, it is likely you will write a final unit for the year's end. As you prepare for your second year of implementation, you can either plan for the first unit at the end of the first year, during the summer, or at the very start of the second year. Keep in mind that each year launches with an introductory period during which routines, procedures, and building ensemble are the focus. The units of study will launch after the introductory period closes.

TABLE 5.2 Sample Rubric

Essential Question: How do submarines help or harm the world?

Task: Design a submarine prototype, role play a conversation between supporters and opponents, then develop and deliver a speech to state legislators convincing them of the need to continue supporting the submarine base.

Standards	Score 1	Score 2	Score 3
ELA Standard: CCSS.ELA-LITERACY.RI.3.3 Describe the relationship between a series of historical events, scientific ideas or concepts, or steps in technical procedures in a text, using language that pertains to time, sequence, and cause/effect. CCSS.ELA-Literacy.W.3.1 Write opinion pieces on topics or texts, supporting a point of view with reasons.	Responds to some or no parts of the prompt. Does not state opinion and/or demonstrates little to no understanding of topic or text(s).	Responds to most parts of the prompt. States opinion that demonstrates understanding of topic or text(s).	Responds skillfully to all parts of the prompt. States opinion that demonstrates an insightful understanding of topic or text(s).
Social Studies Standard: Analyze the impact of geography, economics, and government structures to study the history and contemporary society of Connecticut and local towns.	Demonstrates inaccurate or insufficient analysis of the impact of geography, economics, and government structures to study the history and contemporary society of Connecticut and local towns.	Demonstrates accurate analysis of the impact of geography, economics, and government structures to study the history and contemporary society of Connecticut and local towns.	Demonstrates insightful analysis of the impact of geography, economics, and government structures to study the history and contemporary society of Connecticut and local towns.

(Continued)

TABLE 5.2 (Continued)
Essential Question: How do submarines help or harm the world?

Standards	Score 1	Score 2	Score 3
Science Standard: Define a simple design problem that can be solved through the development of an object, tool, process, or system and include several criteria for success and constraints on materials, time, or cost.	Designs a submersible object using a given set of materials that ascends, descends, or maintains neutral buoyancy.	Designs a submersible object using a given set of materials that ascends and descends.	Designs a submersible object using a given set of materials that ascends, descends, and maintains neutral buoyancy.
Visual Arts Standard: Determine messages communicated by an image.	Does not demonstrate comprehension of the message communicated by an image.	Demonstrates comprehension of the message communicated by an image.	Demonstrates insightful comprehension of the message communicated by an image.
Theatre Standard: Create roles, imagined worlds, and improvised stories in a drama/theatre work.	Creates roles in a drama/theatre work that does not sufficiently convey point of view.	Creates roles in a drama/theatre work that convey point of view.	Creates roles in a drama/theatre work that convey insightful point of view.

TABLE 5.3 Professional Development Timeline

Session Number	Professional Development Session	Suggested Time
PD 1	Foundations of the Work/Setting Up Space	Summer Prior to starting the work
PD 2	Shared Artistic Experience	August
PD 3	Shared Arts Education Experience	September
PD 4	Ensemble Building	September
PD 5	Tableaux	October
PD 6	Pantomime	November
PD 7	Walking in Space	December
PD 8	Improvisation	January
PD 9	Building Integrated Lesson Plans	February
PD 10	Creating Integrated Units of Study	March

Administrative Support

Balancing Support with Accountability

As with the other aspects of the model, leadership will strive to balance supporting the collaborative and creative process of developing units of study with ensuring that staff is accountable for addressing all grade level expectations in rigorous and engaging ways. This process starts with administrative support in terms of scheduling and providing time for co-planning. Planning will either happen after school, during school while hiring substitutes, or ideally by creating standing planning meeting times in the permanent schedule. Demonstrating a commitment to the process sends a strong message of prioritization to teachers.

The integrated units of study are stored in a shared document along with the ensemble activities. This ensures transparency for all; eases the onboarding of new staff; and supports an efficient revision process. The initial development of the units will be time consuming, but it will be well worth the effort. The shared documents also provide leadership a way to cross check that all standards are covered and lessons are planned with fidelity. When it comes time to observe lessons, the shared units of study will become a guidepost and provide context for the work.

Of course, you can expect to see the foundational elements (lesson plans, unit plans, schedule) in place in order to make the work happen. But ultimately, you want to see the impact on students. It is imperative that in the evaluation of the process, you also analyze the learning. Administrators should ensure they are reviewing assessment data, student work samples, and students engaged in the learning process in and out of classrooms. Student achievement and engagement are the ultimate measure of the model's success.

6

Elevating the Role of the Arts Teacher

> Please also consider that with these amazing changes, artistic children from the district will be drawn to [the new school], and some current teachers may not be the most well suited for teaching sensitive, creative, arts inclined children. Training and different approaches to teaching may be necessary to preserve the spirit of an arts centered education. **Parent**

The fourth tenet of the Immersive Arts Integration model is the elevation of the role of the arts specialists in the teaching and learning process. The arts specialists include any teacher who provides direct instruction in the arts including, but not limited to, visual arts, band, strings, vocal music, media arts, theatre, dance, or technology related to the arts. In a traditional school, at best, these teachers may have augmented the learning process by adding a component of their specialty area to core academic content. At worst, these teachers' classrooms served only to allow preparation periods for classroom teachers with little or no regard for their impact on students. In this model, the specialists become an integral part of the planning and learning process. This will require their understanding and acceptance of the expectations and training on how to go about participating in their new roles.

Teachers, Specialists, or Essentialists

What's in a Name?
This chapter is focused on the roles and responsibilities of those who teach the arts in an Immersive Arts Integration model. According to the National Arts Standards, there are five categories of arts: dance, media, music, theatre, and visual arts. It is highly unlikely these five categories will directly correlate to the same number of staff in an elementary or middle school. More often than not, there may be an art teacher and a music teacher who dabble in dance or media, but not all five areas. Sometimes, there are art teachers who teach in uniquely specific genres, such as ceramics or photography. This group of teachers is frequently referred to as "specialists." The Oxford Dictionary defines a specialist as "a person who concentrates primarily on a particular subject or activity; a person highly skilled in a specific and restricted field." On its face, a strings teacher is indeed someone whose singular focus is to teach students to play string instruments. But, this term is limiting in the Immersive Arts Integration model because the art teachers are connected to all learning. Naming the arts as a *special* class connotes that the learning that takes place in that classroom is somehow different from the learning that takes place in an academic classroom setting. Different might mean better, more meaningful, or integral, or it might mean less relevant, separate, or not important. In an Immersive Arts Integration model, arts instruction is not only equally valued but is the vehicle through which learning happens.

Given this context, it is important to use intentionality when referring to those teachers who teach arts. For the purposes of this discussion, they are referred to as arts teachers, so their role is clear to everyone. However, you may want to consider referring to them as "essentialists" or "core teachers." This elevates their role and their subject matter and connotes the arts as a core value of the educational process.

What is Arts Instruction?

Standards Based Arts Instruction

The design of arts instruction for young children means arts teachers follow the district and/or state curriculum based on the National Core Arts Standards. The four standards are creating, performing/presenting/producing, responding, and connecting. Within these are anchor standards that further articulate the concepts. The concepts are applied to the five art forms (dance, music, theatre, visual arts, media arts) using descriptors that increase by complexity based on the grade level. Academic standards are written the same way. The reality is there are inconsistent practices regarding the arts. In some districts, there is a well articulated curriculum with a supervisor that provides professional development, supervision, and accountability measures. In other districts, the curriculum hasn't been revised in decades, and teachers cobble together lesson plans and units based on their understanding of what should be taught. When not grounded in standards, the arts are at risk of devolving into instruction that is low level and not cognitively demanding.

In an Immersive Arts Integration school, it is critical that everyone in the school community recognizes the importance of the arts as a vehicle through which learning takes place. And the arts teachers must be the ones who champion the cause.

Connecting Arts Standards and Academic Standards

Striking Similarities

As of 2018, 44 states require schools to offer arts at the elementary and middle school levels.1 While this is good news, it is unclear which arts are included, how, and how often. This could mean that students have access to a monthly visual arts class after school for art appreciation versus weekly visual arts, music, and theatre classes during which students devise their own works. This allows for a wide range of interpretations of how standards are met. Keep this in mind as you explore ways in which your schools and teams will integrate.

There is a tendency to view academics and arts as separate content areas. There is even a tendency to think of academic content areas as separate. Science instruction happens during the science block, reading instruction happens during the reading block, and music instruction happens during the music block. On the one hand, it is important to isolate content areas to ensure all standards are taught and to highlight skills specific to that discipline. On the other hand, there is also a benefit to integrating subjects. There have been notable efforts in recent years to identify cross curricular connections where possible. Certainly, students read from primary resources during social studies, do math during science, and even demonstrate reading comprehension by creating a poster in art class. There are several instructional models that celebrate integrating the arts with core content, including the Bank Street, HOTS, and Arts Integration and STEAM Implementation Model. Arts integration efforts are well-documented, but it's worth repeating that there is overlap across the standards. When planning is intentional, teams will select relevant standards that serve both the arts and core content curriculum.

Elevating the Role of the Visual Arts and Music Teachers

Roles and Responsibilities

Generally speaking, most schools have a visual arts teacher and one or more music teachers. These arts teachers will participate in the co-planning process on equal footing with the grade level classroom teachers. We will discuss the role of the theatre teacher or arts integration specialists in the next section.

In an Immersive Arts Integration school, the arts are seen as equally valuable as the academics. Therefore, the arts teachers are part of the co-planning process, so they may contribute to the addition of the arts standards in both daily instruction and unit celebrations. In elementary and middle schools, the classroom teacher is responsible for knowing the content in academic

TABLE 6.1 Teachers and Co-Planning Assignments

	Theatre	Visual Arts	Music	Dance	Media Arts
English Language Arts Mathematics Science Social Studies	Art skills taught by the classroom teacher (and the art teacher) using grade level topics identified by the classroom teacher.	Arts skills taught by the art teacher using grade level academic topics identified by the classroom teacher.	Arts skills taught by the art teacher using grade level academic topics identified by the classroom teacher.	Arts skills taught by the art teacher using grade level academic topics identified by the classroom teacher.	Arts skills taught by the art teacher using grade level academic topics identified by the classroom teacher.
	Co-planned and co-taught	Co-planned	Co-planned	Co-planned	Co-planned

areas and the arts teachers in the arts areas. By co-planning, it allows the classroom teacher and the visual arts and music teachers to look for opportunities to integrate the two. It is somewhat common for visual art and music teachers to identify a work of art or a song associated with a story or concept and then challenge students to create their own. The assumption here is that the art teachers are teaching the art skills (painting, drawing, singing, harmonizing, sculpting, etc.), and the classroom teacher is teaching the academic skills (decoding, computation, comprehension, scientific process). The notable exception is in the case of theatre.

Since theatre strategies are such an integral part of the learning process, they are infused throughout the day by the classroom teacher in addition to in the separate theatre class if your school has one. If your school does not have a separate theatre class, you may use a teacher-in-residence model or an after school program with an outsourced provider. The following table articulates who is responsible for the co-planning and instructional processes.

It is quite possible that classroom teachers without a strong arts background may look to the arts teachers as experts in the integration process. However, visual arts and music teachers may be equally inexperienced and/or unprepared or unwilling to shift from planning and teaching within their own room to planning and co-teaching with others. Therefore, it is important to name one's strengths and weaknesses as the work starts and then commit to moving forward together as a unit. Since art teachers may have more of a love for or commitment to their subject areas, they will need to be prepared to bring their colleagues along on the journey.

Elevating the Role of the Theatre Teacher

From Teacher to Arts Integration Coach

In Chapter 2, we discussed the need for a staff member to lead the theatre integration work on an ongoing and sustained basis. It is possible you may hire a new teacher to serve as the Arts Integration Coach; they may already have a theatre background and experience coaching other staff. However, if your scenario involves elevating the role of the theatre teacher to do this work, there will be a shift in practice for this teacher. It is one thing for a teacher to lead students in theatre classes with several ensemble productions over the course of the year, but it is another thing entirely to coach teachers, observe and provide constructive criticism, and lead curriculum writing and content area integration processes. Being a coach requires a unique skill set, knowing the content area, and leading colleagues to improve their practice. Not everyone can make the shift from teacher to coach. The leadership will need to carefully weigh the person who occupies this role as they will be a critical force for positive change in the process. If your theatre teacher transitions to a coaching role, they will need specific professional development on how to coach. Ideally, you can send the teacher for coaching training and provide professional development books. Another option is to provide in-house training from either a math coach, literacy coach, assistant principal, or principal. This training would involve regular sessions to discuss and then model how to coach staff. The trainers should provide frequent feedback as they navigate successful and challenging scenarios.

Professional Development

What Arts Teachers Need to Know

For the purposes of this discussion, we will make the assumption that the arts teachers are certified and/or knowledgeable in their content areas. They have matriculated from a teacher preparation program that provided them with a foundational understanding of art principles and how those apply to teaching their grade levels. They are certainly prepared to teach the content they know and love to their students. However, they may or may not be prepared for or skilled at the co-planning process. Their schema of what it means to be an art teacher may not include sitting in a planning session with a classroom teacher to talk about social studies topics. Arts teachers may welcome this with wild enthusiasm or be unsure of how to support their colleagues or the process. Providing the arts teachers with an ongoing space to connect in their own groups will be very beneficial to the process. Leadership will need to gauge the arts staff to determine where they stand in their beliefs, willingness to evolve, and skill in co-planning. Remember that once you've named your school following an Immersive Arts Integration model, you've made a promise to the community that students will have an experience characterized by the arts; therefore, staff will need to commit to the model as well.

Since the arts teachers come to this work with a perspective different from that of a classroom teacher, it is important they have their own professional development session in advance of creating integrated units of study. During this session, their elevated role is articulated:

- Teach students art skills based on the National Core Arts Standards for their content area
- Plan and execute arts celebrations (concerts, shows, exhibitions, performances)
- Co-plan with classroom teachers. This involves the classroom teacher identifying topic areas and the art teacher identifying artists and projects that align with those topics.

♦ Support the unit celebrations. As discussed in Chapter 5, each unit of study will culminate in a unit celebration that has an arts component. The art teacher(s) will support this process by helping students complete the project where appropriate.

The arts teachers should also attend the same professional development sessions the rest of the faculty and staff attend. It is important everyone understands the model and can support it. It also sends the message that the arts teachers are an integral part of the learning process and are not only included but at the forefront of all school initiatives.

Scheduling Planning Time

Start Slowly, Then Build

Let's be clear: scheduling will be a challenge. There will be approximately five units of study per year. In a K-6 elementary school, this amounts to 30 units of study across all grade levels. If your team is highly effective and able to plan a unit in a half day, this still equates to 15 school days for co-planning for art teachers. You may wish to tackle all of the planning the first year or complete it over a longer period of time. Here are some options for rollout:

♦ Complete the planning process over the summer and make minor revisions during the school year:
  ♦ Pro's: it's complete in advance and does not impact instructional time
  ♦ Con's: teachers may be unavailable, and there may not be funding
♦ Plan after school during the school year:
  ♦ Pro's: it's complete in advance and does not impact instructional time
  ♦ Con's: teachers may be unavailable, and there may not be funding

- Plan during faculty meetings and on professional development days:
  - Pro's: it's complete in advance and does not impact instructional time
  - Con's: this leaves little time for other school initiatives, the days may not align well with the unit calendar; there may not be enough time
- Plan during half or whole day sessions during the school year:
  - Pro's: you can schedule the sessions at beneficial times, and the planning happens immediately in advance of the unit
  - Con's: this impacts instructional time, and substitutes must be funded to cover teachers while they plan
- Plan during regularly scheduled planning sessions (teacher prep times):
  - Pro's: planning happens on a predictable schedule and does not impact academic times
  - Con's: since these typically occur while students have other classes (arts and physical education), it will be difficult to include art teachers

You may also want to consider whether you aim to plan for all units of study in the first year and then revise in subsequent years or plan a portion of the units in year one and then add units in subsequent years. This will depend on time, funding, and many other variables. Your aim should be full implementation by the end of the third year.

Assessing Students' Arts Skills

Subjective Versus Objective

We've discussed formative and summative assessments relative to lessons and units of study. These scores are based on rubrics that were developed to include the art skills. In addition, progress reports or report cards also need to be considered. If your

TABLE 6.2 Sample Fourth Grade Supplementary Progress Report

Standard	Score 1	Score 2	Score 3
Anchor Standard 1: Generate and conceptualize artistic ideas and work.	Student attempts to generate and conceptualize artistic ideas and work by articulating visual details, design elements, improvising stories, and character insight.	Student generates and conceptualizes artistic ideas and work by articulating visual details, design elements, improvising stories, and character insight.	Student generates and conceptualizes comprehensive artistic ideas and work by articulating visual details, design elements, improvising stories, and character insight.
Anchor Standard 2: Organize and develop artistic ideas and work.	Student attempts to collaborate with peers to organize and develop artistic ideas and work.	Student collaborates with peers to organize and develop artistic ideas and work.	Student collaborates with peers to organize and develop comprehensive artistic ideas and work.
Anchor Standard 3: Refine and complete artistic work.	Student attempts to refine and complete artistic work through repetition, collaborative review, and problem solving.	Student refines and completes artistic work through repetition, collaborative review, and problem solving.	Student refines and completes artistic work through repetition, collaborative review, and problem solving that improve the work.
Anchor Standard 4: Select, analyze, and interpret artistic work for presentation.	Student attempts to select, analyze, and interpret artistic work for presentation by modifying dialogue and making physical choices about characters.	Student selects, analyzes, and interprets artistic work for presentation by modifying dialogue and making physical choices about characters.	Student selects, analyzes, and interprets artistic work for presentation by modifying dialogue and making physical choices about characters that improve the work.
Anchor Standard 5: Develop and refine artistic techniques and work for presentation.	Student attempts to develop and refine artistic techniques, including practice exercises in a group setting and the use of technical elements.	Student develops and refines artistic techniques, including practice exercises in a group setting and the use of technical elements.	Student develops and refines insightful artistic techniques, including practice exercises in a group and the use of technical elements.
Anchor Standard 6: Convey meaning through the presentation of artistic work.	Student attempts to convey meaning through the presentation of artistic work in small groups with a peer audience.	Student conveys meaning through the presentation of artistic work in small groups with a peer audience.	Student conveys meaning through the presentation of artistic work to a variety of audiences.

school is part of a district with a pre-existing format, your art school will need to follow this. These reports typically include the arts that all students in the district can access. If your school has additional arts (dance, theatre, etc.) that the other schools do not have, you will also want to capture students' progress in those areas. This is best accomplished through a supplementary progress report that marks progress on the National Core Arts Standards and effort in those areas.

What follows is a sample supplementary fourth grade progress report for theatre based on a trimester schedule and three point scale:

Supervision and Evaluation

Capturing Expanded Expectations Based on the Model

Most districts have a well-articulated teacher evaluation rubric and process. Administrators are required to observe, meet, and provide feedback on this rubric. With the Immersive Arts Integration model, however, there is an added component of co-planning and supporting additional learning celebrations. Every effort should be made to identify and celebrate teachers' efforts to integrate (especially those who have little experience with this). Teaching using an integrated pedagogy is the same as any other type of pedagogy. However, the additional co-planning time and celebrations may feel different (especially in the early phases). Most rubrics have a section that includes professional responsibilities and a section for administrator comments. Be sure to comment on a teacher's progress in this area.

Note

1   https://nces.ed.gov/programs/statereform/tab2_18.asp

7

Spaces and Places

> I applaud [the school] for adding [arts] to the curriculum. Art and music are extremely important to kids' development, and I am extremely grateful that these new programs are being added. I hate that the majority of schools in the USA are cutting these programs; it's a disgrace. Art and music help children to be more rounded and spark creativity and imagination, which is very much needed. **Parent**

The fifth tenet of the Immersive Arts Integration model is the exploration of the spaces and places where art happens across the school campus. Now that you have a sense of what needs to happen, where does it happen? Art traditionally takes place within the four walls of the art room, music room, or on stage. In this model, consider the canvas spanning from curb to curb across the campus. Following are a series of considerations to review to ensure the arts permeate your spaces and places in the most effective way possible.

Infusing the Arts Throughout the School

Impact on Staff and Students

It is important to infuse art both visually and auditorily in every space in and around the building to remind everyone of the school's guiding principles and operating theory. Moving about the educational day in a space that is designed for the purpose will yield the results it was intended to yield for both students and adults. Students' emotional connection to the art will be consistently present because they are surrounded by it daily.

Plan for as many blank spaces as possible. This will invite students to imagine their contributions. There should be empty bulletin boards in classrooms, hallways, and common areas. Research indicates that younger students benefit from uncluttered, visually clean spaces. As students grow and develop, they are able to handle additional visual input. However, our classrooms and schools tend to reflect the opposite. Primary classrooms are filled with busy walls and tons of color that leave students on sensory overload. This is problematic in a traditional school but doubly problematic in an Immersive Arts Integration school. Blank walls and quiet spaces should be filled with artist models and student work as they are produced. A good rule of thumb is that ten percent of the art presented should be an inspirational piece, and ninety percent of the art presented should be from students. This ratio sets the expectation and belief that student art and process are valued and that there is a space for all students to express themselves. Teachers should experiment with having no artist models and/or models from alumni as well.

Evolving the Traditional Classroom

The Classroom as a Safe and Artistic Space

Generally speaking, artistic spaces should foster creativity. There could be soft music playing, comfortable and flexible seating, and a variety of lighting. Elementary classrooms can have stations, and upper elementary and secondary classrooms can have additional access to materials. There is a natural tendency for elementary classrooms to fill with text on walls. This can be overstimulating and not representative of the child's experience. Blank spaces are asked to be filled; they send a message to students that what _they_ create is important.

Consider how students will move about the classroom. There should be flexible seating and various options for creative spaces. The room should feel like a safe space where students can make brave decisions. There should be opportunities for frequent collaboration. Gallery walks will happen frequently, so be sure to leave a path around the perimeter of the room for walking or consider ways to create a path when necessary. Small group collaboration will also happen as students create devised works. There inevitably will be room for seated collaboration, but consider designing pockets of standing spaces where students can connect and collaborate.

Classrooms need dedicated spaces where the art stuff happens. In the classroom context, there is likely to be theatre and

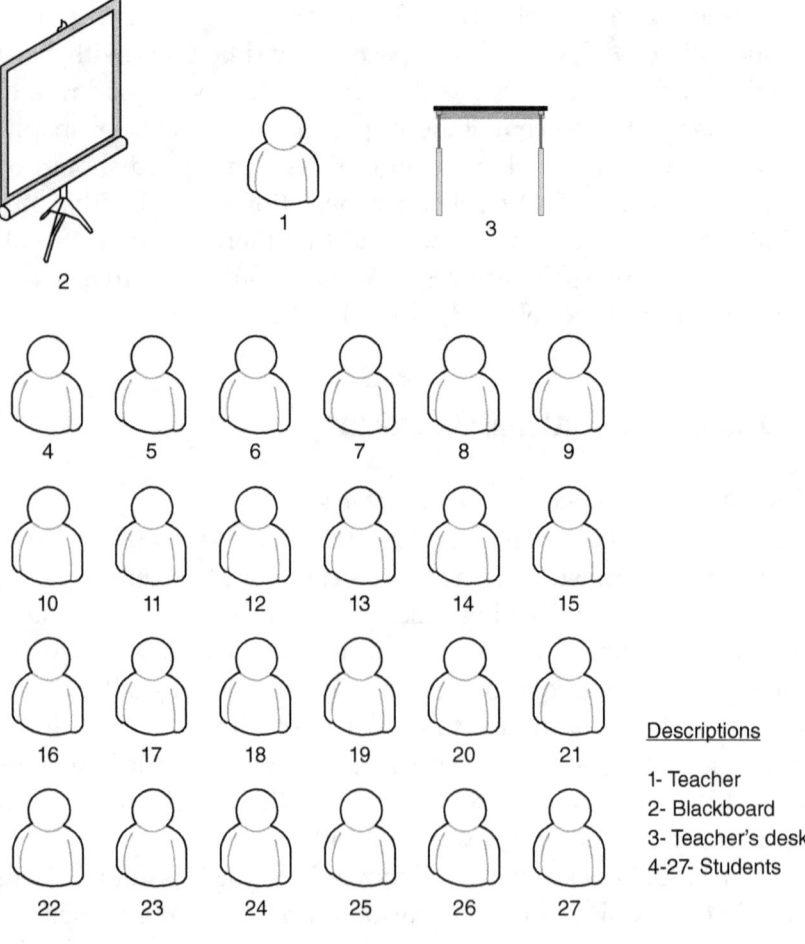

FIGURE 7.1
Example of a traditional classroom design

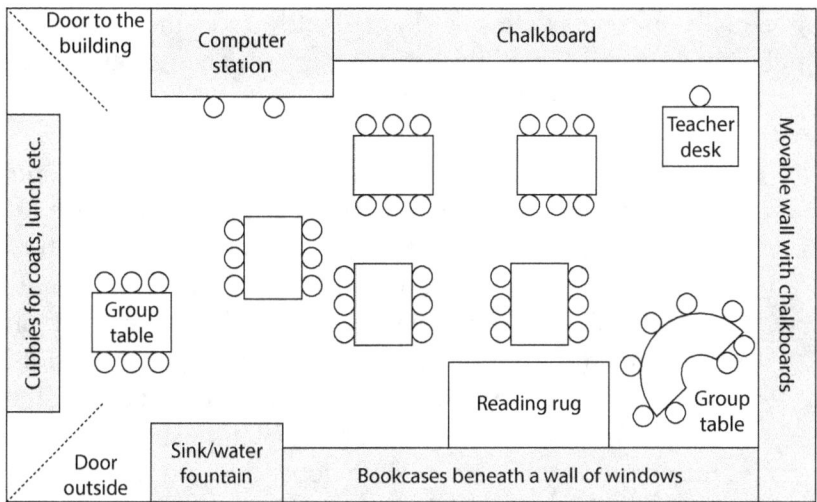

FIGURE 7.2
Example of an Immersive Arts Integration Classroom Design

visual arts components. These spaces should be clearly defined. In terms of visual arts, there should be a clearly labeled place for art materials (crayons, markers, colored pencils, scissors, etc.). These tools should have purpose and meaning throughout instruction. The use of materials should be explicitly taught so that they become easy to use. Most elementary classrooms have writing centers. But, an art corner should become an equally well utilized feature.

Teachers should identify the space in which theatrical instruction and performance will take place. For elementary, a natural choice is on the rug where morning meetings used to happen. For middle or upper elementary, an ensemble may take place after pulling the chairs to the outer walls or pulling them to the center so that theatre can happen in a larger, empty space.

Classroom Design

Teaching Teachers to Design Their Classrooms

As you embark on this journey, it is best to have teachers launch in a way that establishes their ownership over the process and their space. Prior to the school year starting, challenge teachers (especially ones new to this work) to identify and name the spaces in their classrooms where the art will happen. They should identify at least the following spaces:

- Ensemble. This is the place in the room where students will gather at the start and end of each day to launch (at the beginning) and process (at the end) the curriculum work. As discussed in Chapter 3, gathering for ensemble games should take place in a circle so that no one person is more important than the next. The ensemble could take place on a rug so that there is empty space in the middle or around desks that have been pushed together. Ensemble locations can shift depending on the activity that is taking place in that session.
- Arts Center (for supplies and student work). Ideally, you would have a dedicated location to store labeled materials next to a large work table where students could use them. Not all classrooms have this luxury. You may need to store materials when not in use and then take them out when needed. You may push together a group of student desks when needed instead of having a dedicated table. Students may also work on the floor or in the hallway. What is most important is that students have access to a wide variety of materials to demonstrate their learning in creative ways.
- Performance Space. Since there is an emphasis on the use of theatre strategies as a pedagogical tool, the classroom design must include a space for the actors and for the audience. There are traditional "fronts" of rooms, rug space, or other open space designated for this purpose for the performers. The audience can be seated at their desks, on the rug, or stand in a designated location. At the beginning of the process, it is probably a good idea to keep the performance space the same so that students become accustomed to its location. If your performance space requires you to move desks, it will be easier to have one direction that students follow each time you start. Once the process is understood, begin to experiment with

moving locations based on the assignment. It is possible that the classroom performance space is the same as the ensemble space. That's fine; just be intentional about it.
- ♦ Task Display. Students will need a place to display their academic work. This is most often done on a bulletin board. Be sure to leave intentional blank spaces in the classroom; avoid pre-made borders and signage; and give students some autonomy over the decision making process for what to post and when. Projects can also be displayed in the hallway or other common locations throughout the building. Gallery walks (when students are tasked with viewing other student work for specific purposes such as enjoyment, feedback, or learning) should take place frequently.

Beyond the physical components of an integrated arts classroom, there are expectations around the type of work that will take place and how it will take place. While every classroom teacher strives to create a positive climate, in an art integrated space, it is especially important to create the appropriate climate because students will be asked to express themselves in ways that are likely more vulnerable than in a traditional classroom.

Arts Spaces

Considerations for Instruction in Non-Classroom Spaces

Depending on your school's history, you may or may not need to reconsider how space is configured throughout the school building. Most schools built in the 1950s or latter half of the twentieth century were built around the institutional concept that includes an office suite, academic hallways and classrooms, arts rooms, maybe a library, and maybe a gym and separate cafeteria or cafetorium. Consider your spaces, personnel, and learning objectives. What learning do you want to happen, where do you want it to happen, and how do you want it to happen?

Arts instruction will either take place in an art room, classroom, or common area. Ideally, all arts will have an arts space.

A full sized classroom for visual arts, a dance studio for dance, a music room for music, a stage for theatre (in addition to the classroom spaces for theatre), and then smaller spaces for strings or band instruction if those are options at your school. If you do not have dedicated spaces for all these options, the instruction will either need to rotate through a secondary space or rotate in and out of classroom spaces based on a set schedule (this is sometimes referred to as "art on a cart").

Now is a great time for existing art spaces to be re-examined. If you have an art room that's been gathering materials for decades, think about ways to freshen it up and make it feel new and exciting. In terms of materials storage, a good rule of thumb is to give away any materials that can be easily attained through donations. If there is a pile of milk cartons taking up space, send them home with students with a sample list of projects they can do with them; the next time you need milk cartons, ask families to donate them. This is of benefit to students since they will be more invested in a project to which they contributed materials. If you have a music room full of broken instruments, decorate them and hang them on the walls. If there are file cabinets full of copies of old music, send them home with students and keep a master copy electronically to create more space.

If you are adding staff, they will need a home base. Take inventory of the spaces in your building. Note whether there is storage space where supplies gather dust, an annex off the library that is seldom used, or an old locker room that can be converted. There is no shame in converting a storage space into an office space. If the square footage is suitable to house someone with the furniture they need to do their job successfully, the space's original purpose is not relevant. If your stage serves as a storage space for gym equipment, it's time to clear it off. Install shelving in an alternate location or use rolling carts so they can be moved during rehearsal and performances. Ensure the spaces and places in your building are inviting and ready to host and support the learning that will take place.

Schools should aim to have facilities that are able to host the five art forms. Ideally, there would be separate classrooms for music, visual arts, theatre, and dance. Spaces should be able to accommodate at least one full classroom of students. They should be visually appealing and have materials congruent with the art form. Walls can be adorned with a combination of accomplished artists (with care to include diverse examples) and student artwork. Many facilities would be unable to dedicate that amount of real estate to those programs. Sometimes, it takes a little creativity with scheduling, room, and assignments to accommodate the different art forms. Here are some alternatives to consider:

- Part time staff can share a room
- The gym doubles as a dance studio
- Theatre can take place in the cafeteria outside of lunch waves
- Use outdoor spaces

If you find yourself with an unlimited budget, the sky's the limit. Imagine having a recording studio, practice spaces, black box theatre, costumes, or ticket booths. Dream the ideal scenario, and then approximate it to the best of your ability, given your resources and limitations.

Audience

Creating Respectful Recipients

It is important to recognize that performance is an exchange between the performer and the audience. In an elementary or middle school classroom scenario, it also includes the classroom teacher who will evaluate the learning as a result of the performance. We have focused on the role of the performance as reflective of the learning process, but it is equally important for students to learn how to be respectful audience members as well. Here are some key points for teaching students to be audience members:

- Pay attention
- Listen to learn
- Appreciate the performance (this does not mean agree with the performance, rather clap or cheer for the effort)
- Provide feedback to the performer

These skills are not only taught to students but are taught to the adults in the building as well. Performance is not time for teachers to correct papers or text on their phones. Staff should actively be involved as participants in the performance as well.

Professional Development Activity

Classroom Design Collaboration

If your teachers are new to this work, you will need to review and plan for their new classroom design before launching the model. It is important classroom teachers have time and space to visualize how their classrooms will look and what activities will take place in that space. During a professional development session, give teachers each three sheets of paper that can be easily identified (brightly colored paper with some painter's tape or chart paper with adhesive backing). Have them label each paper "ensemble," "art center," and "performance" and list the activities they envision will happen in this space; they can list names of games or other ice breaker activities. They'll post the labels in their classrooms. At this point, the individual teachers will join a small group of colleagues (either on grade level or another configuration) to walk through one another's classrooms. The host teachers can explain to their colleagues their decision making process and why they selected those particular spaces for the activities, and colleagues can offer suggestions or other commentary. The design of this activity allows for a combination of personal planning and reflection followed by collaborative discussion. Including both methodologies increases intentionality and reflection to ensure a strong foundation for future work. Educators always appreciate time and space to connect in less structured ways and places throughout the building. They can have an equally if not more valuable professional development experience when they learn from each other than if they are learning from one knowledgeable other in the worn out faculty meeting space.

Budget

Supporting the Process

Now that teachers can envision what they want in their classrooms, they may need funding to purchase materials for furniture. Classroom art supplies will be necessary for students to integrate the arts on a regular basis. Students will need a space to work with the materials. There are many ways to accomplish these goals, but if you are in need of additional funding, here are some options to consider:

- Build a yearly classroom arts supply into the operating budget and communicate this to teachers so they know how to plan
- Ask a parent organization to raise funds and donate to the arts budget
- Grant write for the arts budget
- Apply for magnet school status or funding
- Develop a GoFundMe list
- Seek donations from the community

In order to create a sustainable program, it is important to develop a system that can be replicated from year to year. All too often, arts funding is the first thing to be cut. Since the arts are the primary vehicle through which learning occurs, your program must be able to sustain prosperous and challenging budget cycles. If you know funds are available from the district, then be sure to build them into your yearly budget as a non-negotiable line item. If you know your parents will need to fundraise, ensure there is a standardized annual appeal and communicate the purpose to the parent community so they know what they are supporting. Grant funding is wonderful, but be sure you have a solid understanding of what and how the funds can be used and have a secondary plan if grant funding is no longer available.

Beyond Stages and Bulletin Boards

Creating Space for Celebrations

In an Immersive Arts Integration model, we encourage arts celebrations every six to eight weeks at the culmination of each unit of study. The development of both units of study and their arts based celebrations were discussed in Chapter 5. These celebrations represent students sharing their learning with an audience. They should take place approximately every six to eight weeks at the end of the units of study. They should be mapped out during the unit planning session and potentially staggered across grade levels to maximize facility usage and resources. Here are some ideas for celebrations:

- Concerts in the hallways as students transition between classes
- Outdoor murals
- Library sculpture installations
- Cafeteria poetry slams

Celebrations are tailored to a specific audience to ensure the success of the performers and audience. Here are some audience ideas for the performance:

- With a friend
- Within a class
- Between classes
- Across the grade level
- Across the school
- With another school
- With parents
- With the community
- With global partners

The performance design will be based on the desired audience and the type of learning that is conveyed. For example, if fifth grade students are tasked with demonstrating their knowledge of changing matter to second grade students, that is best done in a small group live demonstration. If third grade students are tasked with demonstrating their comprehension of a fiction text to the school community, that is best done where the community can access the content (either in a public space or shared electronic platform). Here are some performance method options:

- Live
- Podcast
- Posted on walls
- Local gallery
- Audio
- Website

It is important to note that these unit study celebrations do not take the place of larger scale performances. Students will also participate in the traditional large scale components such as winter concerts, theatre production, and spring art shows. These more traditional performances are time honored traditions and representations of art skills that may or may not be explicitly tied to the curriculum. When scheduling takes place, the team will need to determine the capacity of the art teachers to balance these performances with the unit celebrations and adjust based on the current needs.

8

Implementation in Action

Now that you've learned about the Immersive Arts Integration model, this chapter presents a real life story of how it was implemented in a model school. Here is some demographic information to give you a sense of the context. The school was a K-5 public elementary school in a suburban Connecticut city. The district served approximately 11,000 students in a diverse setting made up of around 50% Hispanic students, 25% White students, 14% Black students, and 11% of students from a combination of other races and nationalities. At this point in history, on the national level, public elementary schools were conceptually and financially competing with charter schools and voucher programs. Don't forget that public schools are funded from local, state, and federal dollars; voucher programs diverted public funds to private or religious schools; and many private schools had themes or other characteristics that were seen as more desirable than what was typically offered at public schools. As a result, many public schools started to develop areas of focus or magnet status to attract families and offer a diversity of choice within a school district. This was the case in the model school's district. The superintendent at the time tasked principals with considering how they might identify an area of focus.

I served as the Principal of the Model Elementary School and was tasked with transitioning it from a school with a traditional approach to education to a school with a focus or theme like several of the other schools in the district. Our school, however, had a much more serious problem. There were persistent rumors that the district was considering closing the school because of its relatively low enrollment as compared to other schools. Our population was less than 300 students and there were other schools in the district with around 550 students. Our immediate neighborhood drew from primarily single family homes, and the population was primarily residents who did not have children. Though we bussed children from other parts of the city, it did little to impact our numbers. Our beloved school, with deep connections to the community, was in danger of closing. We needed a solution, and we needed it fast.

In my mind, the solution was simple: we would transition to a dual language school. Since almost 50% of our students were Hispanic and since there were so many obvious benefits to speaking two languages, this seemed like a natural evolution. I was wrong. My first step was to launch an open conversation with staff to talk about our dilemma. I did not share my thoughts about dual language, rather, I solicited feedback about what they thought made sense. That initial discussion involved staff who had worked in the building anywhere from five to 25 years. One staff member even attended school there as a child, and some had children who attended. Staff talked about what defined the school community and what they valued. Their brainstorming landed on a tradition that had taken place for over 50 years. Every second to the last week of the school year, each grade level rehearsed a song and dance and presented it in a grand celebration to families. The show ended with all grade levels singing one song that inevitably produced tears and roaring applause from the families who had camped out since five that morning to secure spots for their picnic blankets and lawn chairs. The students considered this program to be a gift they presented to the school community. This conversation served as a launch pad for the work ahead. They wanted to be an arts school.

At around the same time, we were the lucky recipients of a local theatre grant for two resident artists to run a program for fifth grade students. One of these artists was Dr. Jennifer Katona, who would later become a partner in the development of the Immersive Arts Integration model. The program design was for three fifth grade classes to devise an original ending to The Three Little Pigs, perform it at the theatre in front of friends and family, and then watch a production of a professional version of the play from a traveling company. The program was wildly popular. Students who were otherwise quiet or had trouble behaving in class were engaged in the process and successful at it. They saw themselves in a new light as they stepped onto the stage to supportive smiles and applause. Families who rarely attended school events carpooled with one another to make it to the performance. The program lasted about two months and then evaporated. It had a clear impact on the students it served, but there was nothing systemic or sustainable about it.

A few short months after the residency, Dr. Katona happened to be in the building and walked by my open office door. I called her in and said, "I want to plant a little seed idea." I shared our staff's preliminary discussions about becoming a school focused on the arts. I told her I didn't want just another school that welcomed short term residencies; I wanted to build a school that used the arts as the primary vehicle through which the learning takes place. I didn't want there to be extra art in the art rooms, I wanted it to be *everywhere*. I asked her if she wanted to be part of the process (although I didn't really know what the process was). She said, "Yes." It was at that moment that the concept of the Immersive Arts Integration model was born.

We were starting to build momentum. The superintendent initiated the idea so he would be on board with whatever direction was established. The staff (who would implement the model) had identified the shift, so most of them were on board. As for me, I had abandoned my idea of a dual language school because it wasn't a fit. Although the arts have always been a huge part of my life from museums to music to performances, I was not an "artist." I didn't have any real talent at drawing or instrumentation or acting or dance. I just had a true appreciation for it all and needed it in my life. I have often struggled with the concept of where and how I fit in a room of artists or leading the charge for an arts school or arts model. But I think the whole point is that art is for everyone and should be in everyone's lives. We should all be champions of the arts because they so closely connect us with

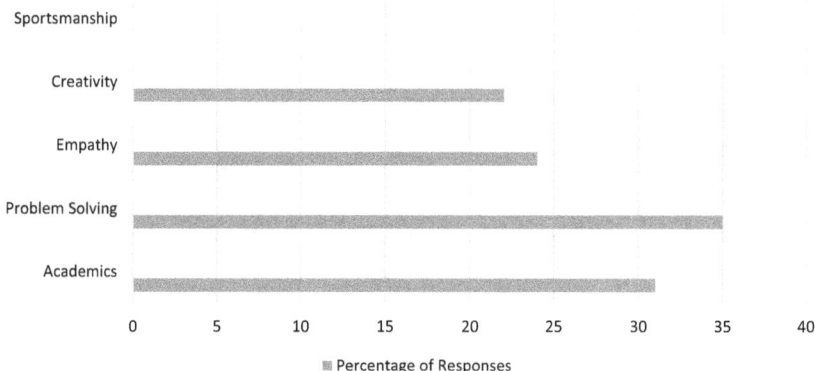

FIGURE 8.1
Parent Survey Responses

our humanity. I appeal to all school leaders to find their places in their respective rooms.

The next step was to solicit input from the school community. The school structure already included a parent advisory board that met monthly. Having this group was a great asset because it allowed me to float ideas to a subset of the parent population in a small group setting and strategically plan for the next steps. At the next meeting, we discussed our declining enrollment dilemma and the fact that teachers were interested in pursuing the arts. The parent group was intrigued by and supported the idea. We decided to launch a series of focus groups and surveys to understand if the broader parent community valued the same things the staff valued and to identify the barriers to the work. The parents helped design the questions. This was a great way to involve them in the process and answer some of the questions that came up in our meetings. The following are the survey questions, results, and a sample of the open ended responses:

The focus groups consisted of several half hour meetings held before, during, and after school with families, school leadership, and two parents from the advisory council. We briefly described some general ideas about a transition to an arts school,

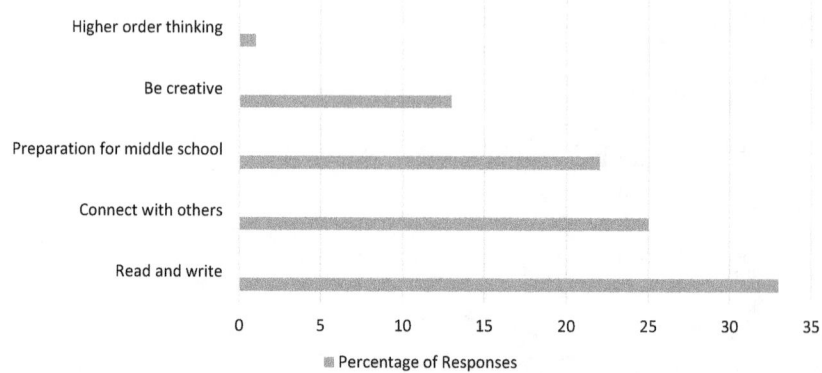

FIGURE 8.2
Parent Survey Responses

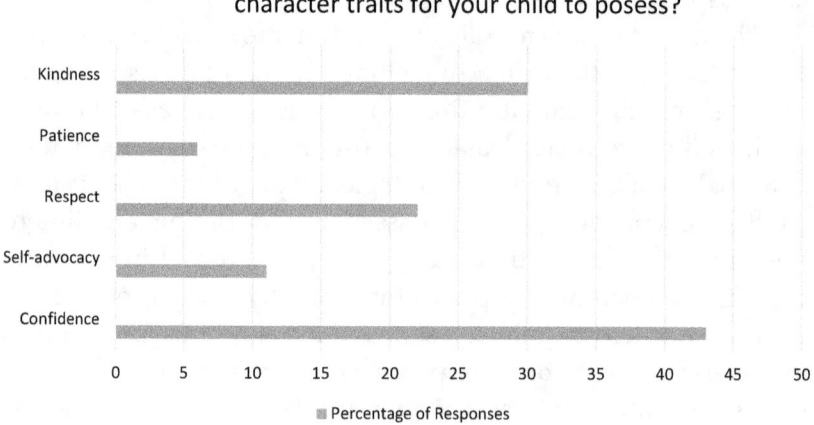

FIGURE 8.3
Parent Survey Responses

Students currently can volunteer for strings lessons in third, fourth, and fifth grades. We are considering offering strings lessons to all students. At what age would you be comfortable with them starting?

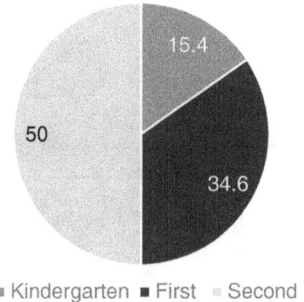

■ Kindergarten ■ First ■ Second

FIGURE 8.4
Parent Survey Responses

Students currently can volunteer for band lessons in third, fourth, and fifth grades. We are considering offering band lessons to all students. At what age would you be comfortable with them starting?

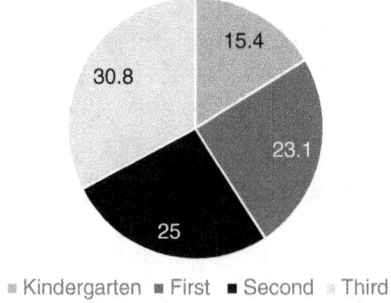

■ Kindergarten ■ First ■ Second ■ Third

FIGURE 8.5
Parent Survey Responses

Students currently can volunteer for band lessons in fourth and fifth grades. We are considering offering band lessons (percussion) in younger grades. What age would you be comfortable starting band?
52 responses

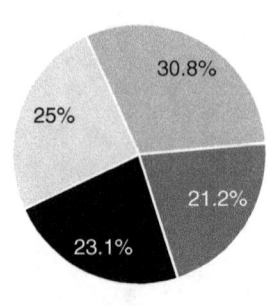

■ Kindergarten ■ First ■ Second ■ Third

FIGURE 8.6
Parent Survey Responses

Survey responses that supported a transition to an immersive arts instruction model

- I'm excited about the potential
- I am excited to see this transition roll out! While I think it will be a great fit for my daughter – I do worry that it may not be the right fit for every student, and that is okay!). I hope that none of the neighborhood students feel like they are being "forced out" if this model does not fit for them. But I also hope that it draws in other students to the community!
- I am so excited about this transition, and you have my support 100%. Yay, arts!
- I am happy to hear we are retaining the physical education program. This is a critical part of the curriculum. While we are looking at changing the schedule, can we see if it is possible to extend recess so that it is longer than 10 minutes? That is not enough time for the kids to get re-energized for the rest of the day.

- I'm thrilled to see the transformation to the arts. It's different and exciting.
- I am excited about the changes happening at [the school]!
- Exciting times
- Excited to see what's to come.
- All good
- We are incredibly excited to see the direction [the school] is going towards. Placing more value on the arts is something we feel very strongly about in our family, and emphasizing the importance of the arts in a child's development is a necessary step in making them well rounded individuals.
- I applaud [the school] for adding these to the curriculum. Art and music are extremely important to kids' development, and I am extremely grateful that these new programs are being added. I hate that the majority of schools in the USA are cutting these programs; it's a disgrace. Art and music help children to be more rounded and spark creativity and imagination. Which is very much needed.
- Incorporating art into traditional academics will be a significant differentiator for [the school] as a school, producing more well rounded, creative, and empathetic students.
- I think it's incredible. It is a very inclusive way for all students. My son is happy especially because he will have the opportunity to learn to play an instrument (which is one of the things that he asks me) apart from dance, and the theatre teaches them a lot to develop as little people.
- Thank you
- In my experience, I've noticed some of the best and brightest students are part of the music programs at [the high school]. Being able to learn an instrument requires work ethic, which goes hand in hand with academic learning.
- I'm sure this will be a wonderful change for the school once we all adjust to it!
- I would love for my daughter to develop the skills she needs in order to be successful. In any area.
- This is a very exciting opportunity for [the school]!

Survey responses that did not support and/or had additional questions about the transition to an Immersive Arts Integration model

- Please consider the sustainable volume of homework across subjects and art classes.
- Will this apply to special needs classes?
- How will this impact my child's basic academic curriculum?
- I would like school to provide a balance in art and academics.
- I'm concerned about the lack of a gym. Kids need that release that they're not going to get from a structured dance class.
- Please also consider that with these amazing changes, artistic children from the district will be drawn to [the school], and some current teachers may not be the most well suited for teaching sensitive, creative, arts inclined children. Training and different approaches to teaching may be necessary to preserve the spirit of an arts centered education.
- I'm worried that PE will be replaced by things like dance. I like that dance will be offered, but feel other physical activities are still very important. I also don't want my child to get to middle school and feel out of place due to all the changes at [the school]. One of the reasons I purchased a home in the area was because of the schools and the community. I hope homeowners like myself are being considered in the decision making process.
- How will the arts affect physical education? Are the traditional areas such as sports and learning team cooperation still be taught?
- String and Band are appropriate at the present grade levels.
- Please continue to send communications regarding the transition. Hoping the additional funding will provide the opportunity to make updates to the school – classrooms, bathrooms, floors, cafeteria, air conditioning.

- I like the addition of Art, Music and Theatre. I question Dance. My daughter loves dance, and we pay separately for it. Dance comes in many forms. So just saying Dance is too vague, and what will be the goal at the end of the class? I also have a son and nephews who aren't into Dance. What would be done to gain their interest? And are you force feeding this or trying to appeal to children who may not have a passion for it?
- Is the increased focus and time on art and music going to add to the already increased amounts of homework every night? The concern is that children will be allowed a more free spirited attitude at school and forced to do hours of homework in the evening. It's already frustrating for parents now as is.
- I'm concerned about sacrificing competency in reading and writing
- Communication on how the arts will be implemented in daily activity – is it taking away from core academics?
- My concern is where the additional 100 students come from. What is the criteria for being admitted if you are not a neighborhood resident? How will all the student needs be met? Our children come in with experience in arts, dance, and music already. Will there be beginner, intermediate, and advanced placement levels? Will more teachers and staff be hired with adding more students? Thanks for your time in reading my comment.
- Whereas I understand the concept of arts integration, the transfer over to an arts magnet school is unnecessary. Yes, there are students whose forte is in the arts, and this should be accommodated by individual teachers to allow for such students to express themselves creatively while others express themselves in a method that best suits their learning and understanding. As was presented in a letter explaining the Arts magnet transition, there was a focus on students learning how to mime their responses. Is this really a skill we want our children to learn? Please tell me how miming responses will prepare my children for

the future. Can this not be integrated into a class as a fun activity or alternate activity to learn a concept rather than be a foundation for class due to an arts focus? I am purely bewildered by this concept of an arts focus! To me, this concept of a magnet school in arts is to serve the purpose of obtaining additional state funds. Why are you going to ruin a school that has been supporting students with well rounded academics to prepare for their future with a concept school that places artistic value in the forefront!?

- If more time is spent in art and music, that is less academic time, which can cause issues later with testing and middle school and high school.
- Generally, this transition sounds like a positive (more funding for the school and a creative outlet for children) – but for those of us living in the [district] who might not otherwise choose an arts magnet program but do want to keep our children at the school (even if it becomes an arts magnet program), it will be important to balance the merits of other elements of the day (gym/physical education/recess immediately come to mind, as fitness and sports are important to us and, I believe, to the health and wellness of all children) with the infusion of more creative subjects – and without shirking on the necessary classroom time for core subjects. I think there is likely a way to balance it all, but I just want to ensure that it is not overlooked – coming from parents who are willing to embrace the arts but don't want their children losing other elements of a balanced school day/curriculum. Thanks!
- I just want to make sure the gym is still one of their specials.
- I want to make sure that physical education does not change in terms of the number of times that students have the class over the course of the week. That is the highlight of my children's day.

then listened as they provided feedback and asked questions. Generally speaking, families were in favor of the transition. They also had a fair amount of questions, which helped guide our next steps. We were sure to address the questions and adapt our approach where necessary. For example, while we initially considered reducing the general physical education time by half and offering dance for the other half, we opted to keep physical education at its current schedule and add dance in addition to it.

In summary, the majority of families were in support of transitioning to an arts school. They valued the arts and saw them as a way to engage students and enhance learning. As a school with almost half its population that received free and reduced lunch, most students did not have the opportunity for extracurricular arts activities after school; parents appreciated that they would not have to pay for costly music or dance lessons. These families in support of the transition wanted more details about how the arts would be integrated and what, if any, academic instructional time would be negatively impacted. There were families who were not in support of the transition. The primary opposition centered around dance in and of itself and dance as it potentially would replace physical education instruction. Families named their biases around dance. In short, they did not believe their boys would want to or should participate in dance because they believed dancing was for girls. In addition, though dance is considered physical education, families wanted their students to learn traditional sports to prepare them for organized and competitive opportunities in middle school and beyond. It was critical to understand both points of view so that questions could be answered and programs could be tailored to meet the community's needs to the greatest extent possible. It was also important to ensure the district would support student transfers if the family truly wanted their child to be elsewhere.

With the support of our superintendent, staff, and school community, the next step was to provide the Board of Education with a status update. The idea was to let them know what was on the horizon and eventually get their approval. Once approved, the schools would receive district funding to support their initiatives. Funding is relative based on a variety of factors;

basically, the funds amounted to our ability to cover 1.5 full time equivalent positions. As with the other groups, the presentation was generally well received. The arts were not terribly controversial, and there were plenty of cultural institutions in the area, so it felt like a good fit. The Board members wanted more specific information about what our programming would look like, but it was yet to be designed. We took it as a win and forged ahead. In the entirety of the process, there were only three official steps that indicated concrete approval from the district: receiving funding, changing the school name, and ensuring the registration process allowed for intradistrict transfers. Since the process was steeped in encouraging participation by the entire school community, responding to all questions and concerns, and bringing people to consensus, it was a very smooth transition that lasted approximately one year.

With a green light from all constituents to transition to an arts school, we needed to identify what that actually looked like. With our foundational commitment to valuing all voices, we wanted staff to identify the characteristics of their newly designed school. We invited them to Dream Big. Staff worked in small groups to list what they thought their school should have and what they thought it should look like. They were encouraged to dream without limits in terms of budget and space. They thought of things like murals, more performances, integrated lessons, theatre, and video productions. They wanted more field trips and exposure to arts outside and inside of the school. We had them go online to research arts schools in the immediate area and beyond. We asked for volunteers to go to local schools with an arts focus to spend a few hours and come back to report their findings to the rest of us. We sent three pairs of teachers to three different schools. Unfortunately, it is somewhat rare to accommodate teacher research. But it was imperative we find out not only what we wanted our new school to look like but what we didn't want it to look like. There was a tremendous amount of buzz around this initiative. We collectively decided each teacher partnership would seek to answer the following questions from their visit:

1. What components are included?
2. What does a normal day look like?

3. How are activities incorporated into the regular education classroom?
4. Does an arts focus impact behavior and test scores?
5. Staff and/or student question: What do you love the most/least about focusing on the arts?
6. What program components do we value?
7. What program components are high leverage?
8. What can we implement fiscally and logistically?

There was lots of talk before, during, and after the trips. Colleagues were excited to hear about the plans and what they found. You could hear a pin drop when staff presented upon their return–everyone was on the edge of their seats, listening for school components that would fit our vision. We took their information and started to plan out some non-negotiables we wanted to include in our program. There was universal agreement about the inclusion of theatre, dance, enhanced strings (including second grade in addition to our current third, fourth, and fifth grade programs), and band (including world drumming for kindergarten through third grade in addition to our current fourth and fifth grade programs). With the components in place, the school leadership team was able to develop a strategic implementation plan that would last the next two years. What you have read in the previous chapters is the articulation of the plan. It included facilities upgrades, materials purchase, staff professional development, and curriculum related initiatives.

The Immersive Arts Integration model was wildly successful. Because there was intentionality in elevating and including the voices of the entire school community, the model's components became inextricably woven into the fabric of the school. The model not only survived but thrived despite the COVID-19 pandemic, a change in principal, and a change in superintendent. After the initial round of professional development coaching cycles on the four theatre strategies, 20 classroom teachers were given a survey so leadership could plan for the next steps. Teachers were asked how comfortable they felt independently incorporating the theatre strategies into their pedagogy. On a five point scale, their answers averaged a 3.6. Teachers were provided with time for integrated arts planning, modeling for peers, and watching peers model for them. Of these strategies, teachers indicated watching their grade level peers was effective. 100% of teachers indicated they wanted to continue with instructional rounds for the remainder of the year. Two-thirds of teachers indicated they wanted to observe teachers from other grade levels teaching the theatre strategies. These positive results indicated that teachers were vested in the professional development process and advocated for it to continue.

The Immersive Arts Integration model was so well received that it was expanded to middle school in the district as well. This shift was initiated differently. The staff of the elementary school identified the arts as a focus, but the middle school was told by the superintendent that this would be their focus. Because it was mandated, there were more staff that were not vested in the process. As Principal, it required me to start with the premise that we did not have a choice in the focus or theme, but the rest of the choices were ours. The middle school was structured differently than the elementary school; the school was divided into three houses that had their own teachers and counselors but shared elective classes. I explained to the staff that we would transition one house to an arts house and allow students and staff to opt into the house. The other two houses would operate under a traditional model. To everyone's surprise, there were so many staff and students who wanted to be in the arts house that we were forced to adjust to two arts houses and one traditional house. The family outreach, professional development, and strategic implementation plan proceeded as it did at the elementary school.

Every school scenario is unique and will have its own set of challenges and characteristics. The intent of the book is to provide you with a framework to use as a point of reference. Once you pass through the initial three year implementation phase, you will add more theatre strategies to teachers' repertoires, refine the curriculum unit plans, and build upon the many ways you infuse art into the educational experience.

Transition Timeline
Preliminary Tasks

- Have stakeholder conversations – Faculty, Staff, Families, Community
- Establish a commitment to transition to an Immersive Arts Integration model

Year 1

- Faculty to complete site visits at like-minded schools
- Identify vision, deliverables, and schedule framework
- Identify professional development needs and providers
- Recruit and hire full time Arts Integration Teacher

Year 2

- Identify materials, facilities upgrades
- Focus on professional development
- Run in-house program at 50%
- Recruit and hire additional arts staff if applicable
- Update mission and vision statements

Year 3

- Rebranding initiative – logo, mural
- Run full inter-district quasi-magnet program with modified bus routes if applicable
- Market to the broad school community
- Recruit students

References

Chapter 1

Ayman-Nolley, S. (1999). Perspective on the dialectic process of creativity. *Creativity Research Journal*, *12*(4), 267–275.

Center for Disease Control. (2022, January). *Guidance for COVID-19 prevention in K-12 schools and ECE programs*. CDC. Retrieved April 9, 2022, from https://www.cdc.gov/coronavirus/2019-ncov/community/schools-childcare/k-12-guidance.html

Center for Disease Control and Prevention. (2022). *Operational guidance for K-12 schools and early care and education programs to support safe in-person learning*. https://archive.cdc.gov/www_cdc_gov/coronavirus/2019-ncov/community/schools-childcare/k-12-childcare-guidance.html

Dewey, J. (1934). *Art as experience*. The Berkley Publishing Group.

Drake, J., & Winner, E. (2012). Confronting sadness through art-making: Distraction is more beneficial than venting. *Psychology of Aesthetics, Creativity, and the Arts*, *6*, 255–261. https://doi.org/10.1037/a0026909

Durlak, J. A., Weissberg, R. P., Dymnicki, A. B., Taylor, R. D., & Schellinger, K. B. (2011). The impact of enhancing students' social and emotional learning: A meta-analysis of school-based universal interventions. *Child Development*, *82*(1), 405–432. https://doi.org/10.1111/j.1467-8624.2010.01564.x

Eisner, E. W. (1998). Does experience in the arts boost academic achievement? *Educational Leadership*, *55*(3), 40–43.

Hiatt, J. (2006). *ADKAR: A model for change in business, government and our community*. Prosci.

Kolb, D. A. (1984). *Experiential learning*. Prentice-Hall.

Kotter, J. P. (1996). *Leading change*. Harvard Business Review Press.

McGregor, D. (1960). *The human side of enterprise*. McGraw-Hill.

McKinsey Quarterly. (2008, March 1). *Enduring ideas: The 7-S framework*. https://www.mckinsey.com/capabilities/strategy-and-corporate-finance/our-insights/enduring-ideas-the-7-s-framework#

United States Department of Education. (2021). *Education in a pandemic: The disparate impacts of COVID-19 on America's students*. https://www.ed.gov/sites/ed/files/about/offices/list/ocr/docs/20210608-impacts-of-covid19.pdf

Zull, J. E. (2002, September). The art of changing the brain. *Educational Leadership*, 68–72.

Chapter 4

Tan, S. (2007). *The arrival*. First edition. Arthur A. Levine Books, an imprint of Scholastic Inc.

For Product Safety Concerns and Information please contact our EU
representative GPSR@taylorandfrancis.com
Taylor & Francis Verlag GmbH, Kaufingerstraße 24, 80331 München, Germany

www.ingramcontent.com/pod-product-compliance
Lightning Source LLC
Chambersburg PA
CBHW061843300426
44115CB00013B/2491